CONTENTS

A DEFENCE OF POETRY

THE FOUR AGES OF POETRY

The Library of Liberal Arts

OSKAR PIEST, FOUNDER

A DEFENCE OF POETRY

Percy Bysshe Shelley

THE FOUR AGES OF POETRY

Thomas Love Peacock

Edited, with an Introduction and notes, by
JOHN E. JORDAN

The Library of Liberal Arts
published by
THE BOBBS-MERRILL COMPANY, INC.
INDIANAPOLIS · NEW YORK

Percy Bysshe Shelley: 1792–1822

Thomas Love Peacock: 1785–1866

Introduction

A BOY throwing rocks can trigger a landslide. Something like that happened when Thomas Love Peacock's "The Four Ages of Poetry" provoked Shelley's "A Defence of Poetry." Peacock was a very clever, very witty "boy," having a good time with a pert squib, obviously agile enough to get out of the way of Shelley's avalanche, but quite outmatched by it. Although Shelley's letters and some of his poems—for example, *Peter Bell the Third* and *The Witch of Atlas*—show that he was not without a sense of humor, he was wont to be intense, and he overlooked the tongue in the cheek of his friend's short satire and responded with a solemn defense more than twice as long, which he still said was only the first part of a three-part document! The history of Shelley's arousal shows the close yet tangential connection between the two essays.

Peacock was a long-time, fairly close and useful friend of the Shelleys. Probably the two men were introduced by Thomas Hookham in 1812, when Shelley mentions reading Peacock's verses.[1] The two writers were frequently together in London during the winter of 1814–1815 and Shelley sent Peacock help when he was imprisoned for debt in 1815.[2] In 1816 Shelley was writing Peacock rich travel letters from Switzerland and with easy confidence commissioning him to take a house in England for the Shelleys, a house that was to be their "fixed, settled, eternal home." [3] Peacock, perhaps wisely, did not assume so onerous a responsibility, and in 1818 he caricatured Shelley's excesses by picturing him as Scythrop in *Nightmare Abbey,* a work which, he explained to the poet, was "to

[1] *The Letters of Percy Bysshe Shelley,* ed. F. L. Jones (Oxford, 1964), I, 333n. Hereafter cited as *Letters.*
[2] *Mary Shelley's Journal,* ed. F. L. Jones (Norman, Okla., 1947), p. 35.
[3] *Letters,* I, 491.

bring to a sort of philosophical focus a few of the morbidities of modern literature, and to let in a little daylight on its atrabilarious complexion." [4] Shelley took this in good part, writing Peacock that he was delighted with the novel and thought the character of Scythrop admirably done.[5] Earlier, on October 14, 1814, Shelley had recorded in Mrs. Shelley's *Journal*: "Peacock calls. I take some interest in this man, but no possible conduct of his would disturb my tranquillity." Perhaps the poet's tranquillity was nevertheless a little disturbed by charges of the "atrabilarious complexion" of modern literature. He would naturally be encouraged to some defense by the rough handling his own poems received from the reviewers and, with more grace, vicariously by the treatment accorded "poor Keats." Significantly, it was probably just before he received Peacock's essay that he wrote a draft of a letter to William Gifford, editor of *The Quarterly Review*, asking not pity for Keats's illness but simple justice for "the very highest style of poetry" in his "Hyperion." [6]

In this mood Shelley awaited with curiosity a box from England bringing the first number of *Literary Miscellany, in Prose and Verse, by Several Hands*, issued in 1820 by his publisher, Charles Ollier, and containing Peacock's "The Four Ages of Poetry." On November 8 Shelley had heard about but not yet seen the piece, and wrote Peacock, "your Essay against the cultivation of poetry has not arrived; my wonder, meanwhile, in what manner you support such a heresy in this matter-of-fact and money-loving age, holds me in suspense." Mary Shelley wrote her friend Maria Gisborne on December 29 asking that the magazine be sent them.[7] By January 20 Shelley had received the box and had been incensed by Peacock's paper, for he then wrote Ollier: "I am enchanted with your *Literary Miscellany*, although the last article it contains has excited my polemical faculties so violently, that

---

[4] *Letters*, II, 30n.

[5] *Letters*, II, 98.

[6] *Letters*, II, 252–253.

[7] *The Letters of Mary W. Shelley*, ed. F. L. Jones (Norman, Okla., 1944), I, 126.

the moment I get rid of my ophthalmia I mean to set about an answer to it, which I will send you, if you please. It is very clever, but, I think, very false." Apparently for a while Shelley thought he would not actually produce the answer, for he wrote Peacock on February 15, blaming not ophthalmia but laziness:

> I received at the same time your printed denunciations against general, and your written ones against particular, poetry [Peacock's letter of December 4: see *Letters,* II, 245n.]; and I agree with you as decidedly in the latter as I differ in the former. The man whose critical gall is not stirred up by such *ottava rimas* as Barry Cornwall's may safely be conjectured to possess no gall at all. The world is pale with the sickness of such stuff. At the same time, your anathemas against poetry itself excited me to a sacred rage, or *caloëthes scribendi* of vindicating the insulted Muses. I had the greatest possible desire to break a lance with you, within the lists of a magazine, in honour of my mistress Urania; but God willed that I should be too lazy, and wrested the victory from your hope; since first having unhorsed poetry, and the universal sense of the wisest in all ages, an easy conquest would have remained to you in me, the knight of the shield of shadow and the lance of gossamere.

Significantly, he asks later in the same letter, "Among your anathemas of the modern attempts in poetry, do you include Keats's 'Hyperion'? I think it very fine." A letter the next day, February 16, to Ollier made no mention of any answer to Peacock.

Yet on February 22, Shelley wrote to Ollier: "Peacock's essay is at Florence at present. I have sent for it, and will transmit to you my paper as soon as it is written, which will be in a few days. Nevertheless, I should be sorry that you delayed your magazine through any dependence on me. I will not accept anything for this paper, as I had determined to write it, and promised it you, before I heard of your liberal arrangements." We may guess that what happened was this: Shelley sent the copy of the *Literary Miscellany* off to Florence to amuse Claire Clairmont, Mary Shelley's stepsister and formerly

Byron's mistress, and might have let the projected reply to Peacock slide if he had not been reminded by Ollier's response to his letter of January 20 that he had more or less promised to supply such an article for the magazine. Now, intending to dash it off in a few days, he went on to tell Ollier in a letter of February 22 that the publisher might expect to receive within a week an essay treating the question "in its elements" and unveiling "the inmost idol of the error." On March 4, however, he was forced to admit to Ollier, "The subject to which the 4 ages of Poetry has provoked my attention requires more words than I have expected; I shall trespass on your patience yet a few days."

Shelley's rough draft—if the quarto notebook in the Bodleian Library (MS Shelley, d. 1) contains that draft, as it appears to—reveals that he got along bumpily with the project. The draft starts off with the general discussion of the roles of reason and the imagination with which the essay finally did begin, but in the third paragraph, just after "because language itself is poetry," the draft is suddenly interrupted by confused versions, full of cancellations and revisions, of a letter to Ollier announcing this essay as an answer to Peacock's. The first draft seemed to be coming out something like this:

Mr. Editor,

The ingenious author of a paper which lately appeared in your Miscellany, entitled the four ages of Poetry, has directed the light of a mind replete with taste & learning to the illustration of [a paradox so dark as itself to absorb whatever rays of truth might fall upon it].

I will endeavour to place the propositions which compose this opinion.

There are four ages of Poetry, corresponding to the four ages of the world [in which this art or faculty has progressively deteriorated] Poetry was at first no more than the rude efforts of expression of man in the dark ages of the world before language had assumed any degree of philosophical perfection; and instead of softening the manners & refining the feelings of the semibarbarians whose intervals of repose it soothed; it flattered their vices

& hardened them to fresh acts of carnage & destruction. The character & personal conduct of the poets themselves, (and this is the most [favourable period? lamentable?] for poetry) was then deserving of contempt.

3dly With the progress of civil society & the developement of the arts of life poetry has deteriorated in exact proportion to the universal amelioration; & the examples in ages of high refinement & civilization & especially by the age in which we live, are below derision, & the instruments of the utmost narrowness & depravity of moral sentiment.

4thly Every person conscious of intellectual power ought studiously to wean himself from the study & the practice of poetry, & ought to apply that power to general finance, political economy, to the study in short of the laws according to which the frame of the social order might be most wisely regulated for the happiness of those whom it binds together.

[These are indeed high objects, & I pledge myself to worship Themis rather than Apollo if I have attempted to, if it could be found that]

Before we subject these propositions to [analysis examination], it were well to discover what poetry is [8]

The text is interrupted by other revisions and additions, including:

So dark a paradox may absorb the brightest rays of mind which fall upon it. [It is an impious daring attempt to extinguish Imagination which is the Sun of life, Impious attempt, parricidal & self murdering attempt] & would leave to its opponent a secure but an inglorious conquest.

He would extinguish Imagination which is the Sun of life, & grope his way by the cold & uncertain & borrowed light of the

[8] In this and the following draft I have ignored all cancellations except those of special interest, which are shown in brackets. For different readings of this difficult manuscript see A. H. Koszul, *Shelley's Prose in the Bodleian Manuscripts* (London, 1910), pp. 118–120; *Peacock's Four Ages of Poetry, Shelley's Defence of Poetry, Browning's Essay on Shelley*, ed. H. F. B. Brett-Smith (Oxford, 1929), pp. 107–110; *The Complete Works of P. B. Shelley*, ed. Roger Ingpen and Walter E. Peck (London, 1926–1930), X, 245–247 (known as the Julian edition, and hereafter cited as *Julian*); and especially, *Letters*, II, 272–274.

Moon which he calls Reason,—stumbling over the interlunar chasm of time where she deserts us, and an owl, rather than an eagle, stare with dazzled eyes on the watery orb which is the Queen of his pale Heaven.—But let us in true sense place within the scale of reason an opinion so light, that there is less danger that it should preponderate, than that the winged words of which it is composed should fly out of the balance like those with which Spensers giant thought to counterpoise the golden weight of Justice. with which this writer attempts to prove that Poetry is a bad thing. [I hope soon to see a Treatise against the light of the Sun adorn your columns—He rides his hobby, like Obadiah did the coach horse through thick & thin, but] He rides his hobby of a paradox with a grace

Dropping the idea of summarizing Peacock's argument, Shelley then tried another draft:

Mr. Editor,

The following remarks were suggested by an essay entitled the Four ages of Poetry which appeared some months since in your valuable Miscellany. [I was delighted by the wit, the spirit, the learning of this essay; but the paradox it attempts to support   I suspect it to be written by a friend of mine who is a desperate rider of a hobby hobbyhorsical   It is impossible not to be delighted   The wit the learning & the spirit of this essay are the spurs of a hobby of a new construction:] but these qualities deserve to be buried, where four roads meet, with a stake through their body, for they are caught in the very fact of suicide. The writer is, in this respect, like a pig swimming, he cuts his own throat.

Did Shelley write the drafts of the letters first and then turn back a few pages in his notebook to start afresh and simply skip over the letters when he came to them—as Brett-Smith thinks—or did he start more solemnly and impersonally and then drop that approach to toy for a while with an epistolary style, only to return to his original tone? Whichever he did, it is clear that early in the composition Shelley tried his hand at the kind of wry treatment Peacock deserved—

comparing him to a dazzled owl, a hobbyhorse rider, and a swimming pig cutting his own throat. But this would not do: Shelley, thinking of Keats and his own work, could not deal so lightly with the subject of poetry. Although he still clung to the notion of having an introductory letter, he pruned it drastically in his third draft, which appears at the end of his fair copy. Since this relatively clean draft suggests that Shelley's essay would have been so prefaced had it appeared in Ollier's journal as he intended, the letter has been placed at the head of the text in this edition.

Somehow Shelley got on with the essay. Mary Shelley's *Journal* shows that she was at work transcribing "A Defence of Poetry" from March 12 to 20, and on the latter date Shelley wrote to Ollier, sending the essay with injunctions which show the importance the poet attached to this work: "I have written nothing which I do not think necessary to the subject. Of course, if any expressions should strike you as too unpopular, I give you the power of omitting them; but I trust you will, if possible, refrain from exercising it. In fact, I hope that I have treated the question with that temper and spirit as to silence cavil. I propose to add two other parts in two succeeding Miscellanies. It is to be understood that, although you may omit, you do not alter or add." A postscript asked Ollier to send a copy of the *Miscellany* containing the essay to Peacock as from the author.[9]

The next day Shelley himself politely informed Peacock that he had entered the lists with him: "I dispatch by this post the 1st Part of an Essay intended to consist of 3 parts, which I design for an antidote to your 'Four Ages of Poetry.' " He went on to admit that his own lance might not be of a matching length and to beg that the contest not fall into the kind of name-calling he had himself played with in his letter drafts: "You will see that I have taken a more general view of what is Poetry than you have, and will perhaps agree with several of my positions without considering your own touched.

[9] *Julian*, VII, 247n.

But read & judge, & do not let us imitate the great founders of the picturesque Mr. Price & Payne Knight,[10] who like two ill-trained beagles began snarling at each other when they could not catch the hare.—"

Then came the long frustrating wait of an author who has worked hard to meet a publishing deadline only to find unexpected delays. Still having heard nothing from Ollier by June 8, Shelley inquired whether his contribution had been received. Apparently he had not given up the intention of writing the other two projected parts of the "Defence," but had done little if anything in that direction, for he told his publisher on September 25: "Pray give me notice against what time you want the second part of my *Defence of Poetry.* I give you this Defence, and you may do what you will with it." Four months later, generally disgusted with Ollier's operations, Shelley gave his London friend John Gisborne wide authority over his affairs, writing him on January 26, 1822: "As also the paper entitled the *Defence of Poetry* over which I gave Ollier the right of insertion in his magazine.—If he declines to insert it, you can do what you will with it—Publish it as a pamphlet."

The reason for the long delay was the failure of Ollier's *Literary Miscellany.* As Gisborne wrote to Shelley on February 19, 1822, the magazine "did not answer." So far it had made only one appearance, and it was never destined to make another. Shelley's essay was held up, however, simply because the editors had not yet surrendered; they still hoped to get out a second number, and they were keeping the "Defence" for that purpose.[11] Shelley, understandably, was in no mood to be tied to the sinking journal; on March 7, 1822, he wrote Gisborne with some asperity: "The Defence of Poetry was not given him [Ollier] to keep two years by him—If he chooses to publish it in a pamphlet (the likeliest form for success) he is welcome; if not I wish it to be sent to me." Nothing more was said about parts two and three. Three months later, when

10 See footnote 11, p. 14.
11 *Letters,* II, 378n.

the "Don Juan" went down in a squall off the coast of Viareggio on July 8, Shelley was drowned—he never finished "A Defence of Poetry," nor ever saw any of it in print.

The "Defence" was next supposed to have been published in *The Liberal,* a journal which Leigh Hunt came to Italy to edit with the support of Shelley and Byron just before Shelley's death. Trying to get the manuscript into the hands of John Hunt, Leigh's brother and publisher of *The Liberal,* Mary Shelley wrote Maria Gisborne on November 6, 1822, asking her to tell Peacock, who somehow had got hold of the essay, to send it to Hunt. By November 26 she was able to report to Maria that she had heard from Hunt's nephew that Peacock had indeed turned over the "Defence" to be published in *The Liberal.*[12] Peacock was later a little miffed that all the allusions to his "Four Ages of Poetry" "were struck out by Mr. John Hunt when he prepared the paper for publication,"[13] and his statement is supported by the circumstantial evidence of the Bodleian transcript in Mary Shelley's hand (MS Shelley, e. 6), which has all but one of these passages canceled in black ink different from that otherwise used.[14] Mary Shelley, however, thought all was going well, and even reported to Trelawney that the "Defence" was published in the second number of *The Liberal,* on January 1, 1823. [15] But she was mistaken. Although *The Liberal* had a brilliant beginning with Byron's *The Vision of Judgement,* it was soon in trouble. Without Shelley as a buffer, Hunt and Byron did not get along well, and the journal expired after four numbers—never printing "A Defence of Poetry." The essay did not in fact appear until late in 1839, when Mary Shelley published it in *Essays, Letters from Abroad, Translations and Fragments* (dated 1840). Peacock complained that because she printed it from Hunt's revised copy the paper stood as a defense without an

[12] *Letters of Mary W. Shelley,* I, 199, 206.

[13] *Peacock's Memoirs of Shelley,* ed. H. F. B. Brett-Smith (London, 1909), p. 208n.

[14] Koszul, p. 61.

[15] *Letters of Mary W. Shelley,* I, 212.

attack. Apparently Mrs. Shelley actually used another transcript than that which John Hunt had marked up, a transcript in her hand which she removed from the notebook that contained Shelley's translation of *The Symposium* and his essay "On Love"; [16] but she did continue to cut out the references to Peacock's essay, as have most subsequent reprints of "A Defence of Poetry." By returning the excised passages to those places where Shelley had them, the present edition puts the defense and attack together.

Peacock's essay is a *tour de force,* a *jeu d'esprit.* As a piece of unified and controlled prose, it outstrips Shelley's "Defence." Peacock builds a diabolical machine, carefully constructed from historical evidence, purporting to be a coolly rational survey of the development of poetry from its primal beginnings, full of neat parallels and witty insights—all so that he can bring it crashingly to attack the poetic productions of his contemporaries. It matters not that the parallels are sometimes undeveloped and the logic occasionally specious; the whole is admirably done. The reader appreciates and is amused by his epigrammatical turns, his air of bluff forthrightness, his clever manipulations, his gradual heightening to the climactically hyperbolical denunciations of nineteenth-century poets.

Peacock's attack upon poetry is not like Stephen Gosson's in the *Schoole of Abuse*—which brought forth Sidney's *Apologie for Poetrie*—on the Puritanical grounds of immorality. Nor is it really, like Plato's in *The Republic,* on the philosophical grounds of inaccuracy. It is rather on the good nineteenth-century grounds of inutility. He sets the tone early in his essay when he accounts for the beginning of poetry in the wish of some chief to be eulogized, lumping it with other trades and making it no more than a commodity that flourished in proportion to the demands of the market. Here is the crux of Shelley's disagreement: he was painfully conscious of the poor market for his own verse—"If Adonais had no success & excited no interest what incentive can I have to write?"

he asked in a letter to Leigh Hunt on January 25, 1822—but he could never admit that the poet plied a trade and produced a commodity. The utility of poetry rested on quite another basis.

The title of Peacock's essay is somewhat misleading. He actually distinguishes eight ages, four classical and four modern, each set going through the sequence iron, gold, silver, and brass. The classical iron age was the bardic period, when poets were relatively close to reality, had a virtual monopoly on the knowledge of the day, and served as historians, theologians, moralists, and legislators. In some sense Shelley would claim that they still are, albeit the "unacknowledged legislators of the world." The gold age was Homeric—retrospective, universal, a marriage of art and truth. By the silver age, the Virgilian epoch, poetry had become civilized and was either content to be monotonously imitative or developed in the direction of the comic, didactic, and satiric. But this state of poetry—he argues with a logic that is short of inevitable—is a certain step toward extinction, because the best vehicle for reason and understanding must be "the simplest and most unvarnished phrase." Hence the world of thought was withdrawn from poets even as that of facts had already been, and poetry perforce declined to the Nonnic age of brass, which professed to return to nature and sought in vain to revive the age of gold by a barbaric verbosity.

The modern iron age of legend and chivalric heroes sprang from the new barbarism of the Dark Ages, in which, according to Peacock's witty exploitation of the paradox, as the light of the Gospel spread over Europe, lo, "by a mysterious and inscrutable dispensation, the darkness thickened with the progress of the light." The Renaissance brought the new gold age of Ariosto and Shakespeare, a hodgepodge compound of various ages and nations all together; and then with Milton—who combined the excellences of both periods—steadied into the reign of authority, the silver age. This authority was shaken by Hume, Gibbon, Rousseau, and Voltaire; Cowper became more concerned with his ideas than with his versification;

and poetry shared in the excited intellectual activity of the
time. Peacock's analysis of the transition to the modern age
of brass is ingenious if not really consistent with his thesis
that a nineteenth-century poet must be "a waster of his own
time and a robber of that of others." He argues that Cowper
and Thomson first really looked at hills and trees, starting
the "Lake Poets" off on their exaggerated pursuit of nature, in
the belief that nothing artificial can be poetical, and mak-
ing contemporary poets semibarbarians, out of place in a
civilized community. When he insists that "barbaric manners
and supernatural interventions are essential to poetry," he
is virtually refuting Wordsworth's contention in the "Pre-
face" to the *Lyrical Ballads* that poetry could be written on
common life, refuting it in terms which are reminiscent of
Coleridge's 1817 description in his *Biographia Literaria* of
Wordsworth's effort to "excite a feeling analogous to the
supernatural, by awakening the mind's attention from the
lethargy of custom, and directing it to the wonders of the
world before us" (Chap. XIV) .

Of course, Peacock has just shown that the age of silver
could produce a "poetry of civilized life" mirroring the "ac-
tivity of the intellect," and he apparently does not consider
that—even if he is right in believing that his contemporaries
are off on a wrong track—poets still have the potential of
looking freshly at many things besides hills and trees, that
their utility lies in their vision. No, he seems to forget that he
has granted poetry itself excellence in past ages, and now
condemns even its finest moments as "the rant of unregulated
passion, the whining of exaggerated feeling, and the cant of
factitious sentiment." If one takes pleasure in the ornamen-
tation of verse, he would do better to read work written in
more poetic ages, but of course any time spent on poetry is
after all taken away from some useful occupation! And there-
fore the productive intellects of the age look down on "Par-
nassus far beneath them, and, knowing how small a place it
occupies in the comprehensiveness of their prospect, smile
at the little ambition and the circumscribed perceptions with

which the drivellers and mountebanks upon it are contending for the poetical palm and the critical chair." So Peacock ends his essay. It is, as Shelley said, clever but false. Shelley could agree that Barry Cornwall (B.W. Procter) was a weak poetaster, but Peacock does not mention him in the essay, as he had privately in a letter to Shelley, or intend to mock only the feeble: he attacks specifically Scott, Byron, Southey, Wordsworth, Moore, Campbell, and Coleridge. Certainly Shelley could find some fault with these, but he likewise found much to admire, and there was also Keats, not to mention the "pardlike Spirit" of Shelley himself. To dismiss all as "drivellers" was a perverse judgment not required by Peacock's thesis, even if that were acceptable, which it was not. No wonder Shelley felt impelled to break a lance.

Peacock had essentially denied the utility of modern poetry because of its irrational character. Shelley tries to show the utility of poetry because of its suprarational character—by a Wordsworthian connection which Shelley never quite makes so specifically, on the ground of the value of the

> . . . Imagination, which, in truth,
> Is but another name for absolute power
> And clearest insight, amplitude of mind,
> And Reason in her most exalted mood.
>
> (*The Prelude*, XIV, 189–92)

Certainly Peacock paid no attention to the great emphasis placed upon the imagination by such contemporaries as Wordsworth, Coleridge, Hazlitt, and Byron. He used the word only once in his essay, and them lumped it with "feeling." Shelley starts by distinguishing the analytic and the synthetic faculties and defining poetry as the latter, as "the expression of the imagination." Thus poetry did not begin in the need to decorate with praise some barbaric chieftain, but it goes back to the origin of mankind, and even language is nothing less than poetry. For all creative ordering of life is poetry, and not only authors but also those who produce music and the dance, architecture, statuary, and painting, and likewise lawgivers, founders of society, inventors of social arts, and religious teachers—all are poets. While Peacock had identified poetry with the primitive and the ornamental, making it an outgrown "mental rattle," Shelley made it the means of apprehending the true, the beautiful, and the good, the agency of human participation in the eternal, the infinite, and the universal. Peacock's conception is bound by time; Shelley's is timeless.

After such a broad introduction, Shelley admits that in a more restricted sense poetry is expressed in language, particularly metrical language. With understandable prejudice he claims superiority for the poetry of language by the questionable assertion that because it deals only with thoughts it is not susceptible to the limitations of materials—which is to give words more tractability and timelessness than they probably have. Denying the popular distinction between prose and verse, he defines the language of poetry as merely harmonious patterns of sound, thus making it possible for him to assert that Plato and Bacon were poets because of the harmony and rhythm of their periods, although they did not use traditional meters. Since parts of a composition can be poetic even when the whole piece is not a poem, he can go so far as to claim that all the great historians were poets.

Having defined poetry, Shelley sets out to "estimate its effects upon society," that is, to meet Peacock on his utilitarian ground—so much so that a 1839 review in *The Spectator* declared that Shelley's essay appeared "to have been written in the heyday of the Utilitarians and Political Economists." [17] Expanding the Aristotelian and Horatian position that poetry pleases and instructs, Shelley asserts that it mingles wisdom and delight in degrees which only the fullness of time can discriminate. An author may find it necessary to make some concessions to the vices of his contemporaries, but nevertheless the proportions of the eternal will show through. For the moral effect of poetry resides not in its ethical teachings but in its stimulus to the imagination: "The great instru-

[17] *Letters of Mary W. Shelley*, II, 143n.

ment of moral good is the imagination; and poetry administers to the effect by acting upon the cause." This is the heart of Shelley's essay, and of much of his other work; it is the crux of his answer to Peacock, the real basis of his "Defence." Following Peacock's survey technique, but not using his four-age chronology, Shelley then loosely skims literary history to show the indirect moral influence of the imagination, arguing that when corruption begins, as in some stages of the drama, poetry ends. Thus the Hellenistic writers can be considered to be connected with the corruption of their age not to the extent that they were poets but only so far as they were *not* poets. It is not the function of poetry to hold a plain mirror up to life, to show distortion, but to use a prismatic mirror that reflects the brightest image of human nature in ideal reality. The great moral principle is that of equality, an imaginative creation of love, which he holds has been the central theme of poets since Plato—Dante, Petrarch, Ariosto Tasso, Shakespeare, Spenser, Calderón, Rousseau. Certainly it is central to Shelley's own poetry. He believed deeply in the power and primacy of love, and in the need for sensitive identification with others. His essay "On Love" defines love as "that powerful attraction towards all that we conceive, or fear, or hope beyond ourselves, when we find within our own thoughts the chasm of an insufficient void, and seek to awaken in all things that are, a community with what we experience within ourselves." [18] In *Epipsychidion*, which ends, "for I am Love's," Shelley makes the connection with the imagination:

> Love is like understanding, that grows bright,
> Gazing on many truths; 'tis like thy light,
> Imagination! which from earth and sky,
> And from the depths of human fantasy,
> As from a thousand prisms and mirrors, fills
> The Universe with glorious beams, and kills

[18] *Shelley's Prose, or the Trumpet of a Prophecy*, ed. David Lee Clark (Albuquerque, N. M., 1954), p. 170. References to Shelley's prose are made to this convenient edition.

Error, the worm, with many a sun-like arrow
Of its reverberated lightning.

(162–69)

Suddenly Shelley interrupts his essay to say, "But let us not be betrayed from a defence into a critical history of Poetry and its Influence on Society." And for a few pages he tries to examine more specifically what Peacock means by utility, recognizing that although anything which supports and purifies the feelings, develops the imagination, and enlivens experience certainly is in some sense useful; nevertheless "The Four Ages" demands a more material sort of usefulness. With this limitation Shelley has little patience; mankind's needs cannot be met by mere facts and inventions: we already know more than we practice and produce more than we have the heart to distribute wisely. Our problem is that "We want the creative faculty to imagine what we know; we want the generous impulse to act that which we imagine."

Surging upward like his own skylark, Shelley rises passionately to the assertion that poetry is no less than divine, that it brings mankind Promethean gifts from sacred precincts forever beyond the calculation of mere reason. It is not, therefore, under the volitional control of the poet, but comes from some external prompting and leaves in the finished work a poor vestige of its conception. This visitation, nevertheless, "turns all things to loveliness" and makes poets the wisest and happiest of men. From this peroration Shelley descends to remark that he has not followed the order of Peacock's arguments but has tried to define poetry more universally. In a second part, he promises, he will apply these principles to the poetry of his own age, which burns with vitality and, he predicts, will be memorable, in spite of the "low-thoughted envy which would undervalue contemporary merit." This ending comes from Shelley's *A Philosophical View of Reform,* probably written in 1819–1820. It reflects the frame of mind which made so irksome Peacock's indiscriminate damning of contemporary poets as "drivellers" and helped to produce "A Defence of Poetry."

Any English poet setting out to write "A Defence of Poetry" would certainly have in mind Sir Philip Sidney's *The Defence of Poesie* or, by its alternative title, *An Apologie for Poetrie*. Any alert nineteenth-century English poet could hardly help but be aware of the interesting views on poetry expressed in Wordsworth's "Preface" to the *Lyrical Ballads,* first published in 1800 but continually reprinted in Wordsworth's collected editions, and in Coleridge's *Biographia Literaria,* which appeared some three years before Shelley wrote his "Defence." Any poet with Shelley's knowledge of the writers of classical antiquity would also think of Aristotle's *Poetics* and Horace's *Ars Poetica,* and especially Plato's famous attack upon poets in *The Republic* as well as his comments on poetry in *The Ion, The Phaedrus,* and *The Symposium.* All of these influences appear in Shelley's essay, as the notes of the text will suggest; but chief of these was probably Plato.

Shelley's standards for keeping up with his reading of Greek are amusingly established by a letter to Thomas Jefferson Hogg on July 25, 1819: "I have of late read little Greek. I have read Homer again and some plays of Aeschylus and Sophocles, and some lives of Plutarch this spring—that is all." In July 1818 he translated *The Symposium,* and when he received Peacock's essay he wrote to his friend: "I was at that moment reading Plato's 'Ion,' which I recommend you to reconsider" (February 15, 1821). Shelley used the views of Plato in *The Ion, The Phaedrus,* and *The Symposium* to refute the charges of Peacock and the Plato of *The Republic.* As James A. Notopoulos remarks, "The Platonism in this essay goes deeper than incidental borrowing." [19] Both the concept and the imagery of Shelley's mystical insight into the divine nature of poetry are Platonic: "It strips the veil of familiarity from the world, and lays bare the naked and sleeping beauty, which is the spirit of its forms"; "to be a poet is to apprehend the true and the beautiful, in a word, the good."

[19] *The Platonism of Shelley: A Study of Platonism and the Poetic Mind* (Durham, N. C., 1949), p. 346.

Shelley echoes Sidney in a number of specific details, such as beginning with a reference to the Greek word for poetry, insisting that poetry is not synonymous with verse, calling Plato a poet and even historians poets, and asserting that poetry is not subject to volitional control. The romantic poet is not so pious, so much concerned with mimesis and the morality of poetry, so full of genre criticism, or so warmly garrulous as the Renaissance poet—there is nothing in the nineteenth-century essay to match Sidney's, "But what? me thinkes I deserve to be pounded, for straying from Poetrie to Oratorie." Shelley's tone is more solemn, his purpose more general, his claims more mystical.

Since Shelley's goal is to defend poetry in general, rather than any special poetic system, his "Defence" is substantially different from Wordsworth's effort in his "Preface" to justify his "experiment" in the *Lyrical Ballads*. Shelley does not, as do Wordsworth in the "Preface" and Coleridge in the *Biographia Literaria*, talk about such technical matters as the role of metrics and the character of poetic diction. In his "Preface" to *The Cenci* (1819) he seems indeed to align himself with Coleridge's position (*Biographia Literaria*, Chap. XVII) that the "real language of men," which Wordsworth tried to draw from rustics, might better be found in the "ordinary, or *lingua communis*": "I entirely agree with those modern critics who assert that in order to move men to true sympathy we must use the familiar language of men. . . . But it must be the real language of men in general and not that of any particular class." Shelley does, however, follow Wordsworth in his conception of the poet as a man "endowed with a more lively sensibility"—a notion that may owe something to Dryden's famous description, in *Of Dramatic Poesy*, of Shakespeare as "the man who . . . had the largest and most comprehensive soul." And it may be that Shelley's idea that poetry "marries exultation and horror, grief and pleasure, eternity and change" and "subdues to union under its light yoke, all irreconcilable things" reflects, as M. T. Solve suggests, Wordsworth's theory that the effect of meter is to control

and make pleasurable the painful excesses of poetic feeling.[20]
Probably the notion is related to Coleridge's familiar dictum
that poetry "reveals itself in the balance or reconciliation of
opposite or discordant qualities" (*Biographia Literaria*, Chap.
XIV). Certainly Shelley could have found his "film of famili-
arity" phrase in the same chapter of the *Biographia Literaria*.
He also shares the views of Wordsworth and Coleridge that
the chief end of poetry is to please and poets are the happiest
and best of men. Shelley's beautiful statement, "A poem is
the image of life expressed in its eternal truth," means approxi-
mately the same as Wordsworth's in the "Preface"—"Poetry is
the image of man and nature"—for earlier in his essay Words-
worth associates poetry with "the permanent forms of nature."
Both authors use the "image" figure in the context of a
discussion of the ideality of poetry as compared to factual
historical writing. The difference in terminology is a charac-
teristic difference between the two poets. Shelley praises "the
ecstasy of the admiration of nature," but puts it after "the de-
light of love and friendship."

Although Shelley's essay is, then, in some sense an occasional
piece deliberately aimed at Peacock's "Four Ages," and con-
ditioned consciously and unconsciously by other attacks on
and defenses of poetry, it is also—as the notes to the text will
show—a ripe synthesis of much that was important to Shelley.
We have already noted that the end of the piece was adapted
from *A Philosophical View of Reform*. His commentary on
Milton's treatment of Satan was partly lifted from his "Essay on
the Devil and Devils." The initial Aeolian harp image Shelley
had used in his "Essay on Christianity," and the final image
of poets as "unacknowledged legislators," may go back, as N.
I. White notes, to 1811, when Shelley sent Elizabeth Hitchener
a copy of George Ensor's *On National Education*, which
pointed out, "It was under the impression of the power of
song that legislators have used poetry to subdue the savage

[20] Melvin T. Solve, *Shelley, His Theory of Poetry* (Chicago, 1927), p. 54.
See *The Poetical Works of Wordsworth*, ed. T. Hutchinson, revised by
E. de Selincourt (Oxford, 1953), p. 739.

nature of the people." [21] More important, the antipathy for didactic poetry expressed in "A Defence" is of a piece with most of Shelley's work since *Queen Mab* and is stated in the "Preface" to *Prometheus Unbound;* his view of the importance of love can be found in his essay "On Love" and is pervasive in his poetry, particularly "The Sensitive Plant," *Prometheus Unbound,* and *Epipsychidion;* his praise of the literature of ancient Greece is consonant with that romantic Hellenism which glows in much of his poetry; his concern for "the principle of equality" shows in his reform efforts from "An Address to the Irish People" to "Hellas"; his contempt for institutional Christianity, and on the other hand his respect for the teachings of Christ, are apparent from his "Essay on Christianity" and his poems from *Queen Mab* to *Prometheus Unbound*; and the whole conception of poetry as "evanescent visitation . . . arising unforeseen and departing unbidden," an "interpenetration of a diviner nature," arresting "the vanishing apparitions which haunt the interlunations of life," the "visitations of the divinity in Man"—all this is certainly the language of the "Hymn to Intellectual Beauty," Shelley's first good poem, written in 1816:

> The awful shadow of some unseen Power
>   Floats though unseen among us,—visiting
>   This various world with as inconstant wing.
>   (1–3)

> Man were immortal, and omnipotent,
> Didst thou, unknown and awful as thou art,
> Keep with thy glorious train firm state within his heart.
>   (39–41)

"Obedient to the light/That shone within his soul" (*Alastor,* 492–493), Shelley in his greatest prose piece claimed for poetry the grand role he sought for himself in the ecstatic agony of the "Ode to the West Wind":

---

[21] Newman Ivey White, *Shelley* (New York, 1940), I, 624–626.

Drive my dead thoughts over the universe
Like withered leaves to quicken a new birth!
And, by the incantation of verse,

Scatter, as from an unextinguished hearth
Ashes and sparks, my words among mankind!

(63–67)

"A Defence of Poetry" is then Shelley's poetic credo, his *Apologia Pro Vita Sua* in prose, as *Prometheus Unbound* was in verse–and both, by his terms, in poetry.

How remarkably poetic are many glowing passages of the "Defence." When Mary Shelley was preparing to publish the essay in her 1840 volume, she declared with justice that it was "truly magnificent," its diction "exquisitely harmonious," and its imagery "grand & vivid." [22] For although Shelley starts off on, and tries frequently to come back to, a prosaic note of reasonable analysis, he cannot stay there. His tone is quite different from Peacock's; the only touch of that style of satire is in the surprising climax: "Let us assume that Homer was a drunkard, that Virgil was a flatterer, that Horace was a coward, that Tasso was a madman, that Lord Bacon was a peculator, that Raphael was a libertine, that Spenser was a poet laureate." Shelley soars rather than snips, and his language soon matches the hyperbole of his thesis: "A poet participates in the eternal, the infinite, and the one," "a poem is the image of life expressed in its eternal truth," "all high poetry is infinite." He turns to glowing metaphors and similies, "Poëtry lifts the veil from the hidden beauty of the world"; it can be "as a meadow-gale of June" or "a fountain for ever overflowing with the waters of wisdom and delight," or "the root and blossom of all other systems of thought," or "a sword of lightning ever unsheathed, which consumes the scabbard that would contain it." Here is the same effulgence of transcendent imagery we are accustomed to find in Shelley's poems: "But mark how beautiful an order

---

[22] *Letters of Mary W. Shelley*, II, 138.

has sprung from the dust and blood of this fierce chaos! how the World, as from a resurrection, balancing itself on the golden wings of knowledge and of hope, has resumed its yet unwearied flight into the Heaven of time. Listen to the music, unheard by outward ears, which is as a ceaseless and invisible wind, nourishing its everlasting course with strength and swiftness."

To a world no stranger to fierce chaos, Shelley's vision of a divine order, of an imaginative transfiguration wrought by the high poetry of love, remains splendidly inspiring. His music still courses with strength and swiftness, for his "Defence of Poetry" is a defense of the life of the creative spirit, a defense of the ideal humanity of man.

JOHN E. JORDAN

Berkeley, California
July 15, 1965

Note on the Text

"The Four Ages of Poetry," by Thomas Love Peacock, was first published, anonymously, in *Ollier's Literary Miscellany, in Prose and Verse, by Several Hands, to be Continued Occasionally*, No. 1, pp. 183–200. It has been several times reprinted, notably in *The Works of Thomas Love Peacock*, ed. Henry Cole, 3 vols. (London, 1875); *Works*, ed. H. F. B. Brett-Smith and C. E. Jones, 10 vols. (London, 1924–1934); an Appendix to Vol. VII of *The Works of Percy Bysshe Shelley*, ed. H. B. Forman (London, 1880); *Shelley, A Defense of Poetry*, ed. Albert S. Cook (Boston, 1890); and *Peacock's Four Ages of Poetry, Shelley's Defence of Poetry, Browning's Essay on Shelley*, ed. H. F. B. Brett-Smith (Oxford, 1921). A late holograph copy and a one-page holographic fragment which have survived present no significant variants. For a collation, see Brett-Smith and Jones, VIII, 494–495.

"A Defence of Poetry," by Percy Bysshe Shelley, was first published in *Essays, Letters from Abroad, Translations and Fragments*, edited by Mary Shelley and dated 1840, although it actually appeared late in 1839. Mrs. Shelley brought out a second edition in 1845, correcting some misprints, and a third edition in 1852. The essay has, of course, been many times reprinted. The annotated editions of Cook and Brett-Smith mentioned above are of special interest, as are also those of Roger Ingpen in the *Julian Shelley* and of David Lee Clark in his edition of *Shelley's Prose* (Albuquerque, N. M., 1954) —to all of which this edition is indebted.

Five manuscript drafts, transcripts, or fragments have survived. These are described by Brett-Smith in his edition and by Roger Ingpen in the *Julian Shelley* (VII, 351). They are, to use Ingpen's designations, as follows:

Manuscript A—Probably Shelley's first draft, now in the Bodleian Library (MS Shelley, d. 1). In *Shelley's Prose in the Bod-*

leian Manuscripts (London, 1910), A. H. Koszul compares it with MS D and prints important variants.

Manuscript B—An incomplete fair copy in Shelley's hand, a Shelley-Rolls manuscript. It is in two sections, the first of which is included in a notebook containing a draft of "Adonais."

Manuscript C—A fragment of a variant text of the passage on two kinds of utility, first published by Harry Buxton Forman, *The Works of Percy Bysshe Shelley* (London, 1880), VII, 130–132.

Manuscript D—A transcript in Mary Shelley's hand which has all but one of the passages referring to "The Four Ages of Poetry" canceled in black ink, probably by John Hunt. Now in the Bodleian Library (MS Shelley, e. 6); printed by Koszul.

Manuscript E—A transcript by Mary Shelley, originally in the volume containing her transcript of Shelley's translation of *The Symposium,* but removed and sent to the printer as copy for the 1840 *Essays;* also from the Shelley-Rolls Collection.

Manuscript F—A transcript in the hand of Claire Clairmont which Buxton Forman says "presents some variations from the printed text," some of which he has adopted silently in his text.

The text of the present edition has been developed chiefly by comparison of the 1840 and 1845 editions with the transcriptions of MSS A and D by Koszul and of MS B by Ingpen. I have followed Ingpen in using Shelley's fair copy (MS B) as the basic text, supplementing it where deficient from the 1845 text, but I have made a few emendations taking cognizance of the 1840 and 1845 editions, Koszul's transcription of MS D, and Forman's collation of the Clairmont transcript and the 1840 and 1852 texts. I have also included in the notes Forman's transcript of MS C and significant variants of MS A from Koszul's edition. Mary Shelley's editorial revisions seem to be, besides dropping references to Peacock, generally the correction of an occasional grammatical error (for example, in agreement of tenses), modernization of spelling ("ancient" for "antient" and "show" for "shew"), and a reduction of many initial capital letters to lower case.

Some of the more interesting differences between the various texts are here recorded in the footnotes. For a fuller listing of variant readings, especially cancellations in MS B, see the notes of the *Julian Shelley*, VII, 352–358.

I am particularly indebted to the Carl and Lily Pforzheimer Foundation, Inc., on behalf of the Carl H. Pforzheimer Library, for their graciousness in allowing me to compare and collate their copy of the 1845 edition with the original edition of 1840 and subsequent editions.

J. E. J.

Abbreviations

Brett-Smith — *Peacock's Four Ages of Poetry, Shelley's Defence of Poetry, Browning's Essay on Shelley,* ed. H. F. B. BRETT-SMITH. Oxford, 1929. The Percy Reprints, No. 3.

Forman — *The Works of Percy Bysshe Shelley,* ed. HARRY BUXTON FORMAN. 8 vols. London, 1880.

Julian — *The Complete Works of P. B. Shelley,* ed. ROGER INGPEN and WALTER E. PECK. 10 vols. London and New York, 1926–1930. Known as the Julian Edition.

Koszul — *Shelley's Prose in the Bodleian Manuscripts,* ed. A. H. KOSZUL. London, 1910.

Letters — *The Letters of Percy Bysshe Shelley,* ed. FREDERICK L. JONES. 2 vols. Oxford, 1964. Most of Shelley's letters referred to can be found in a number of places and identification by date has usually been given, but this admirable edition is the most convenient and complete.

Shelley's Prose — *Shelley's Prose or The Trumpet of Prophecy,* ed. DAVID LEE CLARK. Albuquerque, N. M., 1954.

Sidney — *The Complete Works of Sir Philip Sidney,* ed. ALBERT FEUILLERAT. 3 vols. Cambridge, 1923. References are to Vol. III, which contains *The Defence of Poesie* as published by Ponsonby in 1595. The same year a different text was published by Olney under the title *An Apologie for Poetrie.* The alternative title is sometimes used to distinguish Sidney's work more readily from Shelley's.

Works (Shelley) — *The Complete Poetical Works of Percy Bysshe Shelley,* ed. THOMAS HUTCHINSON. With Introduction and notes by B. P. KURTZ. New York, 1933. Oxford Standard Edition.

Works (Wordsworth) — *The Poetical Works of Wordsworth,* ed. THOMAS HUTCHINSON, revised by E. DE SELINCOURT. London, 1953. Oxford Standard Edition.

THE FOUR AGES OF POETRY

The Four Ages of Poetry

Qui inter haec nutriuntur non magis sapere possunt, quam bene olere qui in culina habitant.[1]

Petronius

POETRY, LIKE the world, may be said to have four ages, but in a different order: the first age of poetry being the age of iron; the second, of gold; the third, of silver; and the fourth, of brass.

The first, or iron age of poetry, is that in which rude bards celebrate in rough numbers the exploits of ruder chiefs, in days when every man is a warrior, and when the great practical maxim of every form of society, "to keep what we have and to catch what we can," is not yet disguised under names of justice and forms of law, but is the naked motto of the naked sword, which is the only judge and jury in every question of *meum* and *tuum*. In these days, the only three trades flourishing (besides that of priest which flourishes always) are those of king, thief, and beggar: the beggar being for the most part a king deject, and the thief a king expectant. The first question asked of a stranger is, whether he is a beggar or a thief: [2] the stranger, in reply, usually assumes the first, and awaits a convenient opportunity to prove his claim to the second appellation.

The natural desire of every man to engross to himself as much power and property as he can acquire by any of the

[1] "Those who are nourished among these things can no more taste than those who live in a kitchen can smell."

[2] See the Odyssey passim: and Thucydides, I, 5. [Peacock's note]. An example of what Peacock means about the *Odyssey* can be found in the greeting Telemachus and company receive at Pylos: "Is yours a business venture, or do you cruise at random like those pirates who quarter the salt waves and risk their souls to profit by what others lose?" (Book III, T. E. Shaw's trans.).

means which might makes right, is accompanied by the no less natural desire of making known to as many people as possible the extent to which he has been a winner in this universal game. The successful warrior becomes a chief; the successful chief becomes a king: his next want is an organ to disseminate the fame of his achievements and the extent of his possessions; and this organ he finds in a bard, who is always ready to celebrate the strength of his arm, being first duly inspired by that of his liquor. This is the origin of poetry, which, like all other trades, takes its rise in the demand for the commodity, and flourishes in proportion to the extent of the market.

Poetry is thus in its origin panegyrical. The first rude songs of all nations appear to be a sort of brief historical notices, in a strain of tumid hyperbole, of the exploits and possessions of a few pre-eminent individuals. They tell us how many battles such an one has fought, how many helmets he has cleft, how many breastplates he has pierced, how many widows he has made, how much land he has appropriated, how many houses he has demolished for other people, what a large one he has built for himself, how much gold he has stowed away in it, and how liberally and plentifully he pays, feeds, and intoxicates the divine and immortal bards, the sons of Jupiter, but for whose everlasting songs the names of heroes would perish.

This is the first stage of poetry before the invention of written letters. The numerical modulation is at once useful as a help to memory, and pleasant to the ears of uncultured men, who are easily caught by sound: and from the exceeding flexibility of the yet unformed language, the poet does no violence to his ideas in subjecting them to the fetters of number. The savage indeed lisps in numbers, and all rude and uncivilized people express themselves in the manner which we call poetical.

The scenery by which he is surrounded, and the superstitions which are the creed of his age, form the poet's mind.[3] Rocks, mountains, seas, unsubdued forests, unnavigable rivers, surround him with forms of power and mystery, which ignorance and fear have peopled with spirits, under multifarious names of gods, goddesses, nymphs, genii, and daemons. Of all these personages marvellous tales are in existence: the nymphs are not indifferent to handsome young men, and the gentlemen genii are much troubled and very troublesome with a propensity to be rude to pretty maidens: the bard therefore finds no difficulty in tracing the genealogy of his chief to any of the deities in his neighbourhood with whom the said chief may be most desirous of claiming relationship.

In this pursuit, as in all others, some of course will attain a very marked pre-eminence; and these will be held in high honour, like Demodocus in the Odyssey, and will be consequently influenced with boundless vanity, like Thamyris in the Iliad.[4] Poets are as yet the only historians and chroniclers of their time, and the sole depositories of all the knowledge of their age; and though this knowledge is rather a crude congeries of traditional phantasies than a collection of useful truths, yet, such as it is, they have it to themselves. They are observing and thinking, while others are robbing and fighting: and though their object be nothing more than to secure a share of the spoil, yet they accomplish this end by intellectual, not by physical, power: their success excites emulation to the attainment of intellectual eminence: thus they sharpen their own wits and awaken those of others, at the same time that they gratify vanity and amuse curiosity. A skilful display of the little knowledge they have gains them credit for the

3 Cf. Shelley, "But a poet considers the vices of his contemporaries as the temporary dress in which his creations must be arrayed, and which cover without concealing the eternal proportions of their beauty" (p. 39).

4 Demodocus was a blind Phaecian bard who moved Ulysses to tears by his songs of Troy (VIII. 521–535). Thamyris was a Thracian poet who challenged the Muses to a contest and was blinded for his presumption (II. 595).

possession of much more which they have not. Their famil-
iarity with the secret history of gods and genii obtains for
them, without much difficulty, the reputation of inspiration;
thus they are not only historians but theologians, moralists,
and legislators: delivering their oracles *ex cathedra,* and being
indeed often themselves (as Orpheus and Amphion) regarded
as portions and emanations of divinity: building cities with
a song, and leading brutes with a symphony; [5] which are only
metaphors for the faculty of leading multitudes by the nose.

The golden age of poetry finds its materials in the age of
iron. This age begins when poetry begins to be retrospective;
when something like a more extended system of civil polity
is established; when personal strength and courage avail less
to the aggrandizing of their possessor and to the making and
marring of kings and kingdoms, and are checked by organized
bodies, social institutions, and hereditary successions. Men
also live more in the light of truth and within the inter-
change of observation; and thus perceive that the agency of
gods and genii is not so frequent among themselves as, to
judge from the songs and legends of the past time, it was
among their ancestors. From these two circumstances, really
diminished personal power, and apparently diminished famil-
iarity with gods and genii, they very easily and naturally
deduce two conclusions: first, That men are degenerated,
and second, That they are less in favour with the gods. The
people of the petty states and colonies, which have now
acquired stability and form, which owed their origin and
first prosperity to the talents and courage of a single chief,
magnify their founder through the mists of distance and tra-
dition, and perceive him achieving wonders with a god or
goddess always at his elbow. They find his name and his ex-
ploits thus magnified and accompanied in their traditionary

[5] H. F. B. Brett-Smith points out that these allusions, although
common enough, suggest that Peacock may have been reading Sidney's
Defence of Poesie: "So as *Amphion,* was sayde to moove stones with his
Poetry, to build *Thebes,* and *Orpheus* to be listned to by beasts, indeed
stonie and beastly people" (p. 4).

songs, which are their only memorials. All that is said of him is in this character. There is nothing to contradict it. The man and his exploits and his tutelary deities are mixed and blended in one invariable association. The marvellous too is very much like a snowball: it grows as it rolls downward, till the little nucleus of truth which began its descent from the summit is hidden in the accumulation of superinduced hyperbole.

When tradition, thus adorned and exaggerated, has surrounded the founders of families and states with so much adventitious power and magnificence, there is no praise which a living poet can, without fear of being kicked for clumsy flattery, address to a living chief, that will not still leave the impression that the latter is not so great a man as his ancestors. The man must in this case be praised through his ancestors. Their greatness must be established, and he must be shown to be their worthy descendant. All the people of a state are interested in the founder of their state. All states that have harmonized into a common form of society, are interested in their respective founders. All men are interested in their ancestors. All men love to look back into the days that are past. In these circumstances traditional national poetry is reconstructed and brought like chaos into order and form. The interest is more universal: understanding is enlarged: passion still has scope and play: character is still various and strong: nature is still unsubdued and existing in all her beauty and magnificence, and men are not yet excluded from her observation by the magnitude of cities or the daily confinement of civic life: poetry is more an art: it requires greater skill in numbers, greater command of language, more extensive and various knowledge, and greater comprehensiveness of mind. It still exists without rivals in any other department of literature; and even the arts, painting and sculpture certainly, and music probably, are comparatively rude and imperfect. The whole field of intellect is its own. It has no rivals in history, nor in philosophy, nor in science. It is cultivated by the greatest intellects of the age, and listened to by all the rest. This is the age of Homer, the golden age of poetry. Poetry has now attained its perfection: it has attained the point which it cannot pass: genius therefore seeks new forms for the treatment of the same subjects: hence the lyric poetry of Pindar and Alcaeus, and the tragic poetry of Aeschylus and Sophocles. The favour of kings, the honour of the Olympic crown, the applause of present multitudes, all that can feed vanity and stimulate rivalry, await the successful cultivator of this art, till its forms become exhausted, and new rivals arise around it in new fields of literature, which gradually acquire more influence as, with the progress of reason and civilization, facts become more interesting than fiction: indeed the maturity of poetry may be considered the infancy of history. The transition from Homer to Herodotus is scarcely more remarkable than that from Herodotus to Thucydides: in the gradual dereliction of fabulous incident and ornamented language, Herodotus is as much a poet in relation to Thucydides as Homer is in relation to Herodotus. The history of Herodotus is half a poem: it was written while the whole field of literature yet belonged to the Muses, and the nine books of which it was composed were therefore of right, as well as of courtesy, superinscribed with their nine names.[6]

Speculations, too, and disputes, on the nature of man and of mind; on moral duties and on good and evil; on the animate and inanimate components of the visible world; begin to share attention with the eggs of Leda and the horns of Io, and to draw off from poetry a portion of its once undivided audience.

[6] Herodotus (484–424? B.C.) divided his *Histories* into nine books, each bearing the name of one of the Muses. Sidney also called attention to this fact and charged that Herodotus "and all the rest that followed him, either stole or usurped of Poetrie" passionate passages, fictional details, and speeches (p. 5). Thucydides, a younger contemporary of Herodotus, wrote a meticulously accurate *History* of the Peloponnesian War; but he also manufactured speeches for his actors, although he made an effort to adhere as closely as possible to the general sense of what was actually said.

Then comes the silver age, or the poetry of civilized life. This poetry is of two kinds, imitative and original. The imitative consists in recasting, and giving an exquisite polish to, the poetry of the age of gold: of this Virgil is the most obvious and striking example. The original is chiefly comic, didactic, or satiric: as in Menander, Aristophanes, Horace, and Juvenal. The poetry of this age is characterized by an exquisite and fastidious selection of words, and a laboured and somewhat monotonous harmony of expression: but its monotony consists in this, that experience having exhausted all the varieties of modulation, the civilized poetry selects the most beautiful, and prefers the repetition of these to ranging through the variety of all. But the best expression being that into which the idea naturally falls, it requires the utmost labour and care so to reconcile the inflexibility of civilized language and the laboured polish of versification with the idea intended to be expressed, that sense may not appear to be sacrificed to sound. Hence numerous efforts and rare success.

This state of poetry is however a step towards its extinction. Feeling and passion are best painted in, and roused by, ornamental and figurative language; but the reason and the understanding are best addressed in the simplest and most unvarnished phrase. Pure reason and dispassionate truth would be perfectly ridiculous in verse, as we may judge by versifying one of Euclid's demonstrations. This will be found true of all dispassionate reasoning whatever, and all reasoning that requires comprehensive views and enlarged combinations. It is only the more tangible points of morality, those which command assent at once, those which have a mirror in every mind, and in which the severity of reason is warmed and rendered palatable by being mixed up with feeling and imagination, that are applicable even to what is called moral poetry: and as the sciences of morals and of mind advance towards perfection, as they become more enlarged and comprehensive in their views, as reason gains the ascendency in them over imagination and feeling, poetry can no longer accompany them in their progress, but drops into the back ground, and leaves them to advance alone.

Thus the empire of thought is withdrawn from poetry, as the empire of facts had been before. In respect of the latter, the poet of the age of iron celebrates the achievements of his contemporaries; the poet of the age of gold celebrates the heroes of the age of iron; the poet of the age of silver re-casts the poems of the age of gold: we may here see how very slight a ray of historical truth is sufficient to dissipate all the illusions of poetry. We know no more of the men than of the gods of the Iliad; no more of Achilles than we do of Thetis; no more of Hector and Andromache than we do of Vulcan and Venus: these belong altogether to po-etry; history has no share in them: but Virgil knew better than to write an epic about Caesar; he left him to Livy; and travelled out of the confines of truth and history into the old regions of poetry and fiction.

Good sense and elegant learning, conveyed in polished and somewhat monotonous verse, are the perfection of the original and imitative poetry of civilized life. Its range is limited, and when exhausted, nothing remains but the *crambe repetita* [7] of common-place, which at length becomes thoroughly wearisome, even to the most indefatigable readers of the newest new nothings.

It is now evident that poetry must either cease to be cul-tivated, or strike into a new path. The poets of the age of gold have been imitated and repeated till no new imitation will attract notice: the limited range of ethical and didactic poetry is exhausted: the associations of daily life in an ad-vanced state of society are of very dry, methodical, unpoetical matters-of-fact: but there is always a multitude of listless idlers, yawning for amusement, and gaping for novelty: and the poet makes it his glory to be foremost among their purveyors.

Then comes the age of brass, which, by rejecting the polish and the learning of the age of silver, and taking a retro-

---

[7] "Cold cabbage warmed up"; that is, stale repetitions.

grade stride to the barbarisms and crude traditions of the age of iron, professes to return to nature and revive the age of gold. This is the second childhood of poetry. To the comprehensive energy of the Homeric Muse, which, by giving at once the grand outline of things, presented to the mind a vivid picture in one or two verses, inimitable alike in simplicity and magnificence, is substituted a verbose and minutely-detailed description of thoughts, passions, actions, persons, and things, in that loose rambling style of verse, which any one may write, *stans pede in uno*,[8] at the rate of two hundred lines in an hour. To this age may be referred all the poets who flourished in the decline of the Roman Empire. The best specimen of it, though not the most generally known, is the Dionysiaca of Nonnus,[9] which contains many passages of exceeding beauty in the midst of masses of amplification and repetition.

The iron age of classical poetry may be called the bardic; the golden, the Homeric; the silver, the Virgilian; and the brass, the Nonnic.

Modern poetry has also its four ages: but "it wears its rue with a difference." [10]

To the age of brass in the ancient world succeeded the dark ages, in which the light of the Gospel began to spread over Europe, and in which, by a mysterious and inscrutable dispensation, the darkness thickened with the progress of the light. The tribes that overran the Roman Empire brought back the days of barbarism, but with this difference, that there were many books in the world, many places in which they were preserved, and occasionally some one by whom they were read, who indeed (if he escaped being burned *pour l'amour de Dieu*,) generally lived an object of mysterious fear, with the reputation of magician, alchymist and astrologer. The emerging of the nations of Europe from this superinduced barbarism, and their settling into

---

8 "Standing on one foot."
9 See footnote 111, p. 61
10 *Hamlet*, IV, v, 183.

new forms of polity, was accompanied, as the first ages of
Greece had been, with a wild spirit of adventure, which, co-
operating with new manners and new superstitions, raised
up a fresh crop of chimaeras, not less fruitful, though far
less beautiful, than those of Greece. The semi-deification
of women by the maxims of the age of chivalry, combining
with these new fables, produced the romance of the middle
ages. The founders of the new line of heroes took the place
of the demi-gods of Grecian poetry. Charlemagne and his
Paladins, Arthur and his knights of the round table, the
heroes of the iron age of chivalrous poetry, were seen through
the same magnifying mist of distance, and their exploits
were celebrated with even more extravagant hyperbole.
These legends, combined with the exaggerated love that per-
vades the songs of the troubadours, the reputation of magic
that attached to learned men, the infant wonders of natural
philosophy, the crazy fanaticism of the crusades, the power
and privileges of the great feudal chiefs, and the holy mys-
teries of monks and nuns, formed a state of society in which
no two laymen could meet without fighting, and in which
the three staple ingredients of lover, prize-fighter, and fana-
tic, that composed the basis of the character of every true
man, were mixed up and diversified, in different individuals
and classes, with so many distinctive excellencies, and under
such an infinite motley variety of costume, as gave the range
of a most extensive and picturesque field to the two great
constituents of poetry, love and battle.

From these ingredients of the iron age of modern poetry,
dispersed in the rhymes of minstrels and the songs of the
troubadours, arose the golden age, in which the scattered
materials were harmonized and blended about the time of
the revival of learning; but with this peculiar difference,
that Greek and Roman literature pervaded all the poetry
of the golden age of modern poetry, and hence resulted a
heterogeneous compound of all ages and nations in one
picture; an infinite licence, which gave to the poet the free
range of the whole field of imagination and memory. This

was carried very far by Ariosto, but farthest of all by Shakespeare and his contemporaries, who used time and locality merely because they could not do without them, because every action must have its when and where: but they made no scruple of deposing a Roman Emperor by an Italian Count, and sending him off in the disguise of a French pilgrim to be shot with a blunderbuss by an English archer. This makes the old English drama very picturesque, at any rate, in the variety of costume, and very diversified in action and character; though it is a picture of nothing that ever was seen on earth except a Venetian carnival.

The greatest of English poets, Milton, may be said to stand alone between the ages of gold and silver, combining the excellencies of both; for with all the energy, and power, and freshness of the first, he united all the studied and elaborate magnificence of the second.

The silver age succeeded; beginning with Dryden, coming to perfection with Pope, and ending with Goldsmith, Collins, and Gray.

Cowper divested verse of its exquisite polish; he thought in metre, but paid more attention to his thoughts than his verse. It would be difficult to draw the boundary of prose and blank verse between his letters and his poetry.

The silver age was the reign of authority; but authority now began to be shaken, not only in poetry but in the whole sphere of its dominion. The contemporaries of Gray and Cowper were deep and elaborate thinkers. The subtle scepticism of Hume, the solemn irony of Gibbon, the daring paradoxes of Rousseau, and the biting ridicule of Voltaire, directed the energies of four extraordinary minds to shake every portion of the reign of authority. Enquiry was roused, the activity of intellect was excited, and poetry came in for its share of the general result. The changes had been rung on lovely maid and sylvan shade, summer heat and green retreat, waving trees and sighing breeze, gentle swains and amorous pains, by versifiers who took them on trust, as meaning something very soft and tender, without much caring what: but with this general activity of intellect came a necessity for even poets to appear to know something of what they professed to talk of. Thomson and Cowper looked at the trees and hills which so many ingenious gentlemen had rhymed about so long without looking at them at all, and the effect of the operation on poetry was like the discovery of a new world. Painting shared the influence, and the principles of picturesqué beauty were explored by adventurous essayists with indefatigable pertinacity.[11] The success which attended these experiments, and the pleasure which resulted from them, had the usual effect of all new enthusiasms, that of turning the heads of a few unfortunate persons, the patriarchs of the age of brass, who, mistaking the prominent novelty for the all-important totality, seem to have ratiocinated much in the following manner: "Poetical genius is the finest of all things, and we feel that we have more of it than any one ever had. The way to bring it to perfection is to cultivate poetical impressions exclusively. Poetical impressions can be received only among natural scenes: for all that is artificial is anti-poetical. Society is artificial, therefore we will live out of society. The mountains are natural, therefore we will live in the mountains. There we shall be shining models of purity and virtue, passing the whole day in the innocent and amiable occupation of going up and down hill, receiving poetical impressions, and communicating them in immortal verse to admiring generations." To some such perversion of intellect we owe that egregious confraternity of rhymesters, known by the name of the Lake Poets; [12] who

11 William Gilpin, *Essay on Picturesque Beauty* (1792); Uvedale Price, *An Essay on the Picturesque, as Compared with the Sublime and the Beautiful* (1794, enlarged 1796); Richard Payne Knight, *An Analytical Inquiry into the Principles of Taste* (1805). See Christopher Hussey, *The Picturesque: Studies in a Point of View* (New York, 1927).

12 The "Lake Poets" were generally taken to include Wordsworth, Coleridge, and Southey, although the three were in many ways different. Peacock's views resemble those of Francis Jeffrey, influential editor of *The Edinburgh Review:* "At other times, the magnitude of these errors— the disgusting absurdities into which they led their feebler admirers, and the derision and contempt which they drew from the more fastidious, even upon the merits with which they were associated, made us wonder

certainly did receive and communicate to the world some of
the most extraordinary poetical impressions that ever were
heard of, and ripened into models of public virtue, too
splendid to need illustration. They wrote verses on a new
principle; saw rocks and rivers in a new light; and remaining
studiously ignorant of history, society, and human nature,
cultivated the phantasy only at the expence of the memory
and the reason; and contrived, though they had retreated
from the world for the express purpose of seeing nature
as she was, to see her only as she was not, converting the
land they lived in into a sort of fairy-land, which they peopled
with mysticisms and chimaeras. This gave what is called a
new tone to poetry, and conjured up a herd of desperate
imitators, who have brought the age of brass prematurely
to its dotage.

The descriptive poetry of the present day has been called
by its cultivators a return to nature. Nothing is more im-
pertinent than this pretension. Poetry cannot travel out of the
regions of its birth, the uncultivated lands of semi-civilized
men. Mr. Wordsworth, the great leader of the returners to
nature, cannot describe a scene under his own eyes without
putting into it the shadow of a Danish boy or the living
ghost of Lucy Gray,[13] or some similar phantastical parturi-
tion of the moods of his own mind.

In the origin and perfection of poetry, all the associations
of life were composed of poetical materials. With us it is
decidedly the reverse. We know too that there are no Dryads
in Hyde-park nor Naiads in the Regent's-canal. But barbaric
manners and supernatural interventions are essential to po-
etry. Either in the scene, or in the time, or in both, it must
be remote from our ordinary perceptions. While the historian
and the philosopher are advancing in, and accelerating, the

---

more than ever at the perversity by which they were retained, and
regret that we had not declared ourselves against them with still more
formidable and decided hostility" (Review of Wordsworth's *Poems, in
Two Volumes, The Edinburgh Review,* XI [October 1807], 215). Cf.
Byron's comments on the "Lakers" in the "Dedication" of *Don Juan.*

13 See Wordsworth's poems, "Lucy Gray" and "The Danish Boy."

progress of knowledge, the poet is wallowing in the rubbish
of departed ignorance, and raking up the ashes of dead sav-
ages to find gewgaws and rattles for the grown babies of the
age. Mr. Scott digs up the poachers and cattle-stealers of
the ancient border.[14] Lord Byron cruises for thieves and pirates
on the shores of the Morea and among the Greek islands.[15]
Mr. Southey wades through ponderous volumes of travels
and old chronicles, from which he carefully selects all that
is false, useless, and absurd, as being essentially poetical; and
when he has a commonplace book full of monstrosities,
strings them into an epic.[16] Mr. Wordsworth picks up village
legends from old women and sextons,[17] and Mr. Coleridge,
to the valuable information acquired from similar sources,
superadds the dreams of crazy theologians and the mysticisms
of German metaphysics, and favours the world with visions
in verse, in which the quadruple elements of sexton, old wo-
man, Jeremy Taylor, and Emanuel Kant, are harmonized
into a delicious poetical compound.[18] Mr. Moore presents
us with a Persian, and Mr. Campbell with a Pennsylvanian
tale,[19] both formed on the same principle as Mr. Southey's
epics, by extracting from a perfunctory and desultory perusal
of a collection of voyages and travels, all that useful investi-
gation would not seek for and that common sense would
reject.

These disjointed relics of tradition and fragments of
second-hand observation, being woven into a tissue of verse,

14 See *Border Minstrelsy* (1802–1803), *The Lay of the Last Minstrel*
(1805), *Lord of the Isles* (1815).

15 See *The Giaour* (1813), *The Bride of Abydos* (1813), *The Corsair*
(1814), *Don Juan* (1819–1824).

16 For example, *Thalaba* (1801), *Madoc* (1805), *The Curse of Kehama*
(1810), *Roderick, the Last of the Goths* (1814).

17 Probably a reference to *The Excursion* (1814).

18 Probably "The Rime of the Ancient Mariner" (1798) and "Christa-
bel" (1816).

19 Thomas Moore, *Lalla Rookh* (1817); Thomas Campbell, *Gertrude
of Wyoming* (1809).

constructed on what Mr. Coleridge calls a new principle [20] (that is, no principle at all), compose a modern-antique compound of frippery and barbarism, in which the puling sentimentality of the present time is grafted on the misrepresented ruggedness of the past into a heterogeneous congeries of unamalgamating manners, sufficient to impose on the common readers of poetry, over whose understandings the poet of this class possesses that commanding advantage, which, in all circumstances and conditions of life, a man who knows something, however little, always possesses over one who knows nothing.

A poet in our times is a semi-barbarian in a civilized community. He lives in the days that are past. His ideas, thoughts, feelings, associations, are all with barbarous manners, obsolete customs, and exploded superstitions. The march of his intellect is like that of a crab, backward.[21] The brighter the light diffused around him by the progress of reason, the thicker is the darkness of antiquated barbarism, in which he buries himself like a mole, to throw up the barren hillocks of his Cimmerian labours.[22] The philosophic mental tranquillity which looks round with an equal eye on all external things, collects a store of ideas, discriminates their relative value, assigns to all their proper place, and from the materials of useful knowledge thus collected, appreciated, and arranged, forms new combinations that impress the stamp of their power and utility on the real business of life, is diametrically the reverse of that frame of mind which poetry inspires, or from which poetry can emanate. The highest inspirations of poetry are resolvable into three ingredients: the rant of unregulated passion, the whining of

[20] In his Preface to "Christabel" Coleridge claimed that the meter was "founded on a new principle: namely, that of counting in each line the accents, not the syllables."

[21] *Hamlet*, II, ii, 206.

[22] The Cimmerians were a half-mythical people, first mentioned in the *Odyssey*, who supposedly lived in perpetual darkness.

exaggerated feeling, and the cant of factitious sentiment: and can therefore serve only to ripen a splendid lunatic like Alexander, a puling driveller like Werter,[23] or a morbid dreamer like Wordsworth. It can never make a philosopher, nor a statesman, nor in any class of life an useful or rational man. It cannot claim the slightest share in any one of the comforts and utilities of life of which we have witnessed so many and so rapid advances. But though not useful, it may be said it is highly ornamental, and deserves to be cultivated for the pleasure it yields. Even if this be granted, it does not follow that a writer of poetry in the present state of society is not a waster of his own time, and a robber of that of others. Poetry is not one of those arts which, like painting, require repetition and multiplication, in order to be diffused among society. There are more good poems already existing than are sufficient to employ that portion of life which any mere reader and recipient of poetical impressions should devote to them, and these having been produced in poetical times, are far superior in all the characteristics of poetry to the artificial reconstructions of a few morbid ascetics in unpoetical times. To read the promiscuous rubbish of the present time to the exclusion of the select treasures of the past, is to substitute the worse for the better variety of the same mode of enjoyment.

But in whatever degree poetry is cultivated, it must necessarily be to the neglect of some branch of useful study: and it is a lamentable spectacle to see minds, capable of better things, running to seed in the specious indolence of these empty aimless mockeries of intellectual exertion. Poetry was the mental rattle that awakened the attention of intellect in the infancy of civil society: but for the maturity of mind to make a serious business of the playthings of its childhood, is as absurd as for a full-grown man to rub his

[23] Probably Alexander the Great, who in the fourth century B.C. nearly realized his ambition of conquering the whole world; and the sentimental hero of Goethe's early romance, *The Sorrows of Young Werther* (1774, revised 1787).

gums with coral, and cry to be charmed to sleep by the jingle of silver bells.

As to that small portion of our contemporary poetry, which is neither descriptive, nor narrative, nor dramatic, and which, for want of a better name, may be called ethical, the most distinguished portion of it, consisting merely of querulous, egotistical rhapsodies, to express the writer's high dissatisfaction with the world and every thing in it, serves only to confirm what has been said of the semi-barbarous character of poets, who from singing dithyrambics and "Io Triumphe," [24] while society was savage, grow rabid, and out of their element, as it becomes polished and enlightened.

Now when we consider that it is not the thinking and studious, and scientific and philosophical part of the community, not to those whose minds are bent on the pursuit and promotion of permanently useful ends and aims, that poets must address their minstrelsy, but to that much larger portion of the reading public, whose minds are not awakened to the desire of valuable knowledge, and who are indifferent to any thing beyond being charmed, moved, excited, affected, and exalted: charmed by harmony, moved by sentiment, excited by passion, affected by pathos, and exalted by sublimity: [25] harmony, which is language on the rack of Procrustes; sentiment, which is canting egotism in the mask of

[24] "Hurrah Triumph," the shout of Roman soldiers following a conquering general in triumphal procession through Rome.

[25] Cf. Jeffrey, "The end of poetry, we take it, is to please—and the name, we think, is strictly applicable to every metrical composition from which we receive pleasure, without any laborious exercise of the understanding. This pleasure, may, in general, be analyzed into three parts— that which we receive from the excitement of Passion or emotion—that which is derived from the play of Imagination, or the easy exercise of Reason—and that which depends on the character and qualities of the Diction" (*The Edinburgh Review*, XI [October 1807], 216). Contrast Wordsworth: "In the higher poetry, an enlightened Critic chiefly looks for a reflection of the wisdom of the heart and the grandeur of the imagination. Wherever these appear, simplicity accompanies them" ("Essay, Supplementary to the Preface," 1815 [*Works*, p. 743]).

refined feeling; passion, which is the commotion of a weak
and selfish mind; pathos, which is the whining of an un-
manly spirit; and sublimity, which is the inflation of an
empty head: when we consider that the great and permanent
interests of human society become more and more the main
spring of intellectual pursuit; that in proportion as they be-
come so, the subordinacy of the ornamental to the useful
will be more and more seen and acknowledged; and that
therefore the progress of useful art and science, and of moral
and political knowledge, will continue more and more to
withdraw attention from frivolous and unconducive, to solid
and conducive studies: that therefore the poetical audience
will not only continually diminish in the proportion of its
number to that of the rest of the reading public, but will
also sink lower and lower in the comparison of intellectual
acquirement: when we consider that the poet must still please
his audience, and must therefore continue to sink to their
level, while the rest of the community is rising above it: we
may easily conceive that the day is not distant, when the de-
graded state of every species of poetry will be as generally
recognized as that of dramatic poetry has long been: [26] and
this not from any decrease either of intellectual power, or
intellectual acquisition, but because intellectual power and
intellectual acquisition have turned themselves into other and
better channels, and have abandoned the cultivation and the
fate of poetry to the degenerate fry of modern rhymesters,
and their olympic judges, the magazine critics, who continue
to debate and promulgate oracles about poetry, as if it were
still what it was in the Homeric age, the all-in-all of intel-
lectual progression, and as if there were no such things in

[26] Wordsworth argues rather that "A dramatic Author, if he write
for the stage, must adapt himself to the taste of the audience, or they
will not endure him," but "partial notice only, or neglect, perhaps long
continued, or attention wholly inadequate to their merits" has been the
fate of "most works in the higher departments of poetry," for each
great and original author must create "the taste by which he is to be
enjoyed" ("Essay, Supplementary to the Preface," [Works, pp. 744–745,
750]).

existence as mathematicians, astronomers, chemists, moralists, metaphysicians, historians, politicians, and political economists, who have built into the upper air of intelligence a pyramid, from the summit of which they see the modern Parnassus far beneath them, and, knowing how small a place it occupies in the comprehensiveness of their prospect, smile at the little ambition and the circumscribed perceptions with which the drivellers and mountebanks upon it are contending for the poetical palm and the critical chair.

A DEFENCE OF POETRY

Mr. Editor,

The following remarks, which I have presumed to call a Defence of Poetry, were suggested by an Essay of great ingenuity and wit which appeared some time since in your valuable Miscellany; entitled the 'Four Ages of Poetry.' The object of that paper seems to be to persuade the world that Poetry, as Lance says of Conscience 'ought to be driven out of all towns and cities as a dangerous thing.' [1] I entreat, Mr. Editor, to be heard on suspension of judgement.

I remain

Your constant reader

S.[2]

---

[1] The Second Murderer in Shakespeare's *Richard the Third* says that conscience "is turn'd out of towns and cities for a dangerous thing" (I, vi, 145–146). Shelley is apparently confusing this speech with a speech about conscience by Launcelot Gobbo in *The Merchant of Venice* (II, ii, 1–34).

[2] I have normalized this letter in an approximation of the way it probably would have appeared in print had Shelley's essay been published in Ollier's *Miscellany*. For a transcription of the few variants, see *Letters*, II, 274.

A Defence of Poetry [1]

PART I

ACCORDING TO one mode of regarding those two classes of mental action, which are called reason and imagination, the former may be considered as mind contemplating the relations borne by one thought to another, however produced; and the latter, as mind acting upon those thoughts so as to colour them with its own light, and composing from them, as from elements, other thoughts, each containing within itself the principle of its own integrity. [2] The one is the τὸ ποιεῖν, or

[1] MS D has a canceled subtitle: "or Remarks suggested by an Essay entitled 'the four Ages of Poetry'" (Koszul, p. 62).

[2] The language of the following fragments, first printed by Richard Garnett (*Relics of Shelley* [London, 1862], pp. 88–89), suggests that in an early draft Shelley began to discuss imagination in terms of the psychology of associationism, which had been popularized by David Hartley (*Observations on Man, his Frame, Duty and Expectations*, 1749) and was still important in English and Scottish philosophy and exercised considerable influence on the work of Coleridge, Wordsworth, Keats, and Hazlitt.

> In one mode of considering these two classes of action of the human mind which are called reason and imagination, the former may be considered as mind employed upon the relations borne by one thought to another, however produced, and imagination as mind combining the elements of thought itself. It has been termed the power of association; and on an accurate anatomy of the functions of the mind, it would be difficult to assign any other origin to the mass of what we perceive and know than this power. Association is, however, rather a law according to which this power is exerted than the power itself; in the same manner as gravitation is a passive expression of the reciprocal tendency of heavy bodies towards their respective centres. Were these bodies conscious of such a tendency, the name which they would assign to that consciousness would express the cause of gravitation; and it were a vain inquiry as to what might be the cause of that cause. Association bears the same relation to imagination as a mode to a source of action: when we look upon shapes in the fire or the clouds and imagine to ourselves the resemblance of familiar objects,

25

the principle of synthesis, and has for its objects those forms which are common to universal nature and existence itself; the other is the τὸ λογιζειν,[3] or principle of analysis, and its action regards the relations of things,[4] simply as relations; considering thoughts, not in their integral unity, but as the algebraical representations which conduct to certain general results. Reason is the enumeration of quantities already known; imagination is the perception of the value of those quantities, both separately and as a whole. Reason respects the differences, and imagination the similitudes of things.[5] Reason is to imagination as the instrument to the agent, as the body to the spirit, as the shadow to the substance.

Poetry, in a general sense, may be defined to be "the expression of the imagination": and poetry is connate with the origin of man. Man is an instrument over which a series of external and internal impressions are driven, like the alternations of an ever-changing wind over an Aeolian lyre,[6] which move it by their motion to ever-changing melody. But there is a principle within the human being, and perhaps within all sentient beings, which acts otherwise than in the lyre, and produces not melody, alone, but harmony, by an inter-

---

we do no more than seize the relation of certain points of visible objects, and fill up, blend together . . .

The imagination is a faculty not less imperial and essential to the happiness and dignity of the human being, than the reason.

It is by no means indisputable that what is true, or rather that which the disciples of a certain mechanical and superficial philosophy call true, is more excellent than the beautiful.

3 The Greek words mean "making" and "reasoning," respectively. The first is the source of the English word "poet," as Sidney noted: "It commeth of this word *Poiein*, which is to make" (p. 7).

4 MS A: relations of thoughts.

5 Wordsworth defined at least one kind of reason as "that false secondary power/ By which we multiply distinctions" and imaginations as "observation of affinities/ In objects where no brotherhood exists/ To passive minds" (*The Prelude*, II, 216–217, 384–386). Shelley, early influenced by William Godwin, Helvetius, and Holbach, continues to give reason an important, if not an equal, role.

6 MS A: lute.

nal [7] adjustment of the sounds or motions thus excited to the impressions which excite them. It is as if the lyre could accommodate its chords to the motions of that which strikes them, in a determined proportion of sound; even as the musician can accommodate his voice to the sound of the lyre.[8] A child at play by itself will express its delight by its voice and motions; and every inflexion of tone and every gesture will bear exact relation to a corresponding antitype in the pleasurable impressions which awakened it; it will be the reflected image of that impression; and as the lyre trembles and sounds after the wind has died away, so the child seeks, by prolonging in its voice and motions the duration of the effect, to prolong also a consciousness of the cause. In relation to the objects which delight a child, these expressions are, what poetry is to higher objects.[9] The savage (for the savage is to ages what the child is to years) expresses the emotions produced in him by surrounding objects in a similar manner; and language and gesture, together with plastic or pictorial imitation, become the image of the combined effect of those objects, and of his apprehension of them. Man in society, with all his passions and his pleasures, next becomes the object of the passions and pleasures of man; an additional class of emotions produces an augmented treasure of expressions; and language, gesture, and the imitative arts, become at once the representation and the medium, the pen-

[7] MS A: instinctive.

[8] Similarly Wordsworth wrote of feeling "within/ A correspondent breeze" (*The Prelude,* I, 34–35). For a discussion of the popular romantic figure of the Aeolian harp, see M. H. Abram's essay, "The Correspondent Breeze: A Romantic Metaphor," *English Romantic Poets,* ed. M. H. Abrams (Oxford, 1960), pp. 37–54. David Lee Clark (*Shelley's Prose,* p. 277n.) calls attention to Shelley's comparable statement in the "Essay on Christianity": "There is a Power by which we are surrounded, like the atmosphere in which some motionless lyre is suspended, which visits with its breath our silent chords at will." Cf. also Coleridge's "The Aeolian Harp."

[9] MS A: In relation to the ideas of which a child is capable, these expressions are what poetry is to higher ideas (Koszul, p. 64n.).

cil and the picture, the chisel and the statue, the chord and the harmony. The social sympathies, or those laws from which, as from its elements, society results, begin to develop themselves from the moment that two human beings coexist; the future is contained within the present as the plant within the seed; and equality, diversity, unity, contrast, mutual dependence, become the principles alone capable of affording the motives according to which the will of a social being is determined to action, inasmuch as he is social; and constitute pleasure in sensation, virtue in sentiment, beauty in art, truth in reasoning, and love in the intercourse of kind. Hence men, even in the infancy of society, observe a certain order in their words and actions, distinct from that of the objects and the impressions represented by them, all expression being subject to the laws of that from which it proceeds.[10] But let us dismiss those more general considerations which might involve an inquiry into the principles of society itself,[11] and restrict our view to the manner in which the imagination is expressed upon its forms.

In the youth of the world, men dance and sing and imitate natural objects, observing in these actions, as in all others, a certain rhythm or order. And, although all men observe a similar, they observe not the same order, in the motions of the dance, in the melody of the song, in the combinations of language, in the series of their imitations of natural objects. For there is a certain order or rhythm belonging to each of these classes of mimetic representation, from which the hearer and the spectator receive an intenser and purer pleasure than from any other: [12] the sense of an approximation to this order

[10] This is the concept of organic unity and inward determination expressed particularly by Coleridge in the *Biographia Literaria:* "nothing can permanently please, which does not contain in itself the reason why it is so, and not otherwise" (Chap. XIV).

[11] MS A pursues this point: Civil society results from a conflict between these laws & the principle of destruction which accompanies them (Koszul, p. 66n.).

[12] MS A suggests a serene quality in this order: For there is a certain order & rhythm from which a keener & a purer delight results, & within

has been called taste by modern writers.[13] Every man in the infancy of art, observes an order which approximates more or less closely to that from which this highest delight results: but the diversity is not sufficiently marked, as that its gradations should be sensible, except in those instances where the predominance of this faculty of approximation to the beautiful (for so we may be permitted to name the relation between this highest pleasure and its cause) is very great. Those in whom it exists in excess are poets, in the most universal sense of the word; and the pleasure resulting from the manner in which they express the influence of society or nature upon their own minds, communicates itself to others, and gathers a sort of reduplication from that community.[14] Their language

---

which all the intelligent faculties of man gather into a more calm repose, *come fiera in lustra* [as a beast within its lair] (Koszul, p. 66*n.*).

[13] In 1818 William Hazlitt published "Thoughts on Taste" in the *Edinburgh Magazine*, in which he defined genius as "the power of producing excellence" and taste as "the power of perceiving the excellence thus produced" (Herschel Baker, *William Hazlitt* [Cambridge, Mass., 1962], p. 305*n.*). Coleridge wrote a fragment of an "Essay on Taste" in 1810 and in "Essays on the Principles of Genial Criticism" (1814) defined taste as "the intermediate faculty which connects the active with the passive powers of our nature, the intellect with the senses" (*Biographia Literaria*, ed. J. Shawcross [London, 1958], II, 227). Interestingly, he ascribed the same intermediate function to the imagination in the *Biographia Literaria*, Chap. VII. Problems facing "modern writers" on taste were the questions of how far it was active, how far passive, how far personal, how far universal. Archibald Alison (*Essays on the Nature and Principles of Taste*, 1790) sometimes treats taste as passive sympathy, and Wordsworth objected to the passive connotation of the term ("Essay, Supplementary to the Preface," 1815). Shelley seems to accept the universal view of taste set forth by his early favorite, David Hume ("Of the Standard of Taste," 1757) and supported in one way or other by Edmund Burke (*A Philosophical Enquiry into the Origin of Our Ideas of the Sublime and Beautiful*, 1757), Alexander Gerard (*Essay on Taste*, 1759), Lord Kames (*Elements of Criticism*, 1762), and Coleridge, who argued " 'de gustibus' is by no means the same as 'de gustu' " (Shawcross, II, 236).

[14] Cf. Wordsworth: "What is a Poet? . . . He is a man speaking to men: a man, it is true, endowed with more lively sensibility, more enthusiasm and tenderness, who has a greater knowledge of human nature,

is vitally metaphorical; that is, it marks the before unapprehended relations of things and perpetuates their apprehension, until the words which represent them, become, through time, signs for portions or classes of thoughts instead of pictures of integral thoughts; and then if no new poets should arise to create afresh the associations which have been thus disorganised, language will be dead to all the nobler purposes of human intercourse.[15] These similitudes or relations are finely said by Lord Bacon to be "the same footsteps of nature impressed upon the various subjects of the world" [16] —and he considers the faculty which perceives them as the storehouse of axioms common to all knowledge. In the infancy of society every author is necessarily a poet, because language itself is poetry; and to be a poet is to apprehend the true and the beautiful, in a word, the good which exists in the relation, subsisting, first between existence and perception, and secondly between perception and expression. Every original language near to its source is in itself the chaos of a cyclic poem: the copiousness of lexicography and the distinc-

_____

and a more comprehensive soul, than are supposed to be common among mankind; a man pleased with his own passions and volitions, and who rejoices more than other men in the spirit of life that is in him, delighting to contemplate similar volitions and passions as manifested in the goings-on of the Universe" ("Preface" to the _Lyrical Ballads_ [_Works_, p. 737]).

15 This is essentially the position on figurative language which Wordsworth expressed in his 1802 Appendix to the "Preface": "The earliest poets of all nations generally wrote from passion excited by real events; they wrote naturally, and as men: feeling powerfully as they did, their language was daring, and figurative. In succeeding times, Poets, and Men ambitious of the fame of Poets, perceiving the influence of such language, and desirous of producing the same effect without being animated by the same passion, set themselves to a mechanical adoption of these figures of speech, and made use of them, sometimes with propriety, but much more frequently applied them to feelings and thoughts with which they had no natural connection whatsoever. A language was thus insensibly produced, differing materially from the real language of men in _any situation_" (_Works_, p. 741).

16 _De Augment. Scient._, cap. I, lib. iii [Shelley's note].

tions of grammar are the works of a later age, and are merely the catalogue and the form of the creations of poetry.[17]

But poets, or those who imagine and express this indestructible order, are not only the authors of language and of music, of the dance and architecture, and statuary, and painting; they are the institutors of laws, and the founders of civil society, and the inventors of the arts of life, and the teachers, who draw into a certain propinquity with the beautiful and the true, that partial apprehension of the agencies of the invisible world which is called religion. Hence all original religions are allegorical, or susceptible of allegory, and, like Janus, have a double face of false and true.[18] Poets, according to the circumstances of the age and nation in which they appeared, were called, in the earlier epochs of the world, legislators, or prophets: [19] a poet essentially comprises and unites both these characters. For he not only beholds intensely the present as it is, and discovers those laws according to which present things ought to be ordered, but he beholds the future in the present, and his thoughts are the germs of the flower and the fruit of latest time. Not that I assert poets to be prophets in the gross sense of the word, or that they can foretell the form as surely as they foreknow the spirit of events:

17 MS A adds: It was reserved to the present epoch, for Philosophy to illustrate the most astonishing results of metaphysical enquiry . . . and that analogy & even unity in all thoughts & objects of thought, the perception of which is poetry, the expression of which is art, & the application of which to knowledge & use, is invention, has become recognized . . . they are all streams deriving from the same source, & meeting in the same sea, so much that even Criticism, Taste or the science of beauty in art, has been rescued by an appeal to these principles, from the indolence of scepticism (Koszul, p. 68*n*.).

18 MS A adds: those who read the Theogony of Hesiod or the fragments of Orpheus with this persuasion, it is poetry & mythology of the very highest order; to those who read it without this persuasion it is a dull catalogue of epithets & proper names (*ibid.*).

19 Sidney pointed out that "among the *Romanes* a Poet was called *Vates*, which is as much as a diviner, fore-seer, or Prophet" and went on "to shewe the reasonablenesse of this word *Vatis*" (p. 6).

such is the pretence of superstition, which would make poetry an attribute of prophecy, rather than prophecy an attribute of poetry. A poet participates in the eternal, the infinite, and the one; as far as relates to his conceptions, time and place and number are not. The grammatical forms which express the moods of time, and the difference of persons, and the distinction of place, are convertible with respect to the highest poetry without injuring it as poetry; and the choruses of Aeschylus, and the book of Job, and Dante's Paradise, would afford, more than any other writings, examples of this fact, if the limits of this essay did not forbid citation. The creations of sculpture, painting, and music, are illustrations still more decisive.

Language, colour, form, and religious and civil habits of action, are all the instruments and materials of poetry; they may be called poetry by that figure of speech which considers the effect as a synonyme of the cause.[20] But poetry in a more restricted sense expresses those arrangements of language, and especially metrical language, which are created by that imperial faculty, whose throne is curtained within the invisible nature of man. And this springs from the nature itself of language, which is a more direct representation of the actions and passions of our internal being, and is susceptible of more various and delicate combinations, than colour, form, or motion, and is more plastic and obedient to the control of that faculty of which it is the creation. For language is arbitrarily produced by the imagination, and has relation to thoughts alone; but all other materials, instruments, and conditions of art, have relations among each other, which limit and interpose between conception and expression. The former is as a mirror which reflects, the latter as a cloud which enfeebles, the light of which both

[20] Cf. Plato in *The Symposium:* "Poetry; which is a general name signifying every cause whereby anything proceeds from that which is not, into that which is; so that the exercise of every inventive art is poetry, and all such artists poets. Yet they are not called poets, but distinguished by other names" (Shelley's translation, *Plato's Banquet,* ed. Roger Ingpen [1931], p. 80).

are mediums of communication. Hence the fame of sculptors, painters, and musicians, although the intrinsic powers of the great masters of these arts may yield in no degree to that of those who have employed language as the hieroglyphic of their thoughts, has never equalled that of poets in the re- stricted sense of the term; as two [21] performers of equal skill will produce unequal effects from a guitar and a harp. The fame of legislators and founders of religions, so long as their institutions last, alone seems to exceed that of poets in the restricted sense; but it can scarcely be a question, whether, if we deduct the celebrity which their flattery of the gross opinions of the vulgar usually conciliates, together with that which belonged to them in their higher character of poets, any excess will remain.

We have thus circumscribed the meaning of [22] the word Poetry within the limits of that art which is the most familiar and the most perfect expression of the faculty itself. It is necessary, however, to make the circle still narrower, and to determine the distinction beteween measured and unmea- sured language; for the popular division into prose and verse is inadmissible in accurate philosophy.

Sounds as well as thoughts have relation both between each other and towards that which they represent, and a perception of the order of those relations has always been found connected with a perception of the order of the re- lations of thoughts. Hence the language of poets has ever affected a certain [23] uniform and harmonious recurrence of sound, without which it were not poetry, and which is scarcely less indispensable to the communication of its influence,[24] than the words themselves, without reference to that peculiar order. Hence the vanity of translation; [25] it

21 MS B begins here.

22 Only MS B has: the meaning of.

23 1840, Forman: sort of.

24 MS B: action.

25 MS B has canceled after "translation": for it is not translation to create anew.

were as wise to cast a violet into a crucible that you might discover the formal principle of its colour and odour, as seek to transfuse from one language into another the creations of a poet. The plant must spring again from its seed, or it will bear no flower—and this is the burthen of the curse of Babel.

An observation of the regular mode of the recurrence of this harmony in the language of poetical minds, together with its relation to music, produced metre, or a certain system of traditional forms of harmony of language.[26] Yet it is by no means essential that a poet should accommodate his language to this traditional form, so that the harmony, which is its spirit, be observed. The practice is indeed convenient and popular, and to be preferred, especially in such composition as includes much form and action: [27] but every great poet must inevitably innovate upon the example of his predecessors in the exact structure of his peculiar versification. The distinction between poets and prose writers is a vulgar error.[28] The distinction between philosophers and poets has been anticipated. Plato was essentially a poet— the truth and splendour of his imagery, and the melody of his language, is the most intense that it is possible to conceive.[29]

[26] MS D, 1840, 1845, Forman: harmony and language. MS A adds but cancels: But a person, who shall possess in a very limited degree the spirit of poetry, may model his language to the external form of metre; without the spirit [and on the next page] Not but that many poets (and I smile because the reader will smile:—at the apparent paradox resulting from the incommensurability of popular and philosophical language)—have written in metre (Koszul, p. 72n.).

[27] MS D, 1840, 1845, Forman: much action.

[28] Sidney had insisted, "Verse being but an ornament and no cause to Poetrie, sith there have been many most excellent Poets that never versified, and now swarme many versifiers that need never answere to the name of Poets" (p. 10). Wordsworth adds a footnote to his "Preface" to point out that "much confusion has been introduced into criticism by this contradistinction of Poetry and Prose, instead of the more philosophical one of Poetry and Matter of Fact, or Science" (*Works*, p. 736n.).

[29] Sidney had said as much, and had gone on to undermine Plato's famous banishing of poets from his Republic: "So as *Plato*, banishing

He rejected the measure of the epic, dramatic, and lyrical forms, because he sought to kindle a harmony in thoughts divested of shape and action, and he forbore to invent any regular plan of rhythm which should include, under determinate forms, the varied pauses of his style. Cicero sought to imitate the cadence of his periods, but with little success. Lord Bacon was a poet.[30] His language has a sweet and majestic rhythm, which satisfies the sense, no less than the almost superhuman wisdom of his philosophy satisfies the intellect; it is a strain which distends, and then bursts the circumference of the hearer's [31] mind, and pours itself forth together with it into the universal element with which it has perpetual sympathy. All the authors of revolutions in opinion are not only necessarily poets as they are inventors, nor even as their words unveil the permanent analogy of things by images which participate in the life of truth; but as their periods are harmonious and rhythmical, and contain in themselves the elements of verse; being the echo of the eternal music. Nor are those supreme poets, who have employed traditional forms of rhythm on account of the form and action of their subjects, less capable of perceiving and teaching the truth of things, than those who have omitted that form. Shakspeare, Dante, and Milton (to confine ourselves to modern writers) are philosophers of the very loftiest power.

A poem is the image [32] of life expressed in its eternal truth. There is this difference between a story and a poem, that a story is a catalogue of detached facts, which have no other

the abuse, not the thing, not banishing it, but giving due honour unto it, shall be our Patron, and not our adversarie" (p. 34). Cf. also Shelley's Preface to his translation of *The Symposium:* "Plato exhibits the rare vision of close and subtle logic, with the Pythian enthusiasm of poetry."

30 See the *Filium Labyrinthi* and the *Essay on Death* particularly [Shelley's note].

31 MS D, 1840, 1845, Forman: reader's.

32 MS D, 1840, 1845, Forman: very image. Wordsworth defined poetry as "the image of man and nature" ("Preface," *Works,* p. 737).

bond of connexion [33] than time, place, circumstance, cause and effect; the other is the creation of actions according to the unchangeable forms of human nature, as existing in the mind of the creator, which is itself the image of all other minds. The one is partial, and applies only to a definite period of time, and a certain combination of events which can never again recur; [34] the other is universal, and contains within itself the germ of a relation to whatever motives or actions have place in the possible varieties of human nature. Time, which destroys the beauty and the use of the story of particular facts, stript of the poetry which should invest them, augments that of Poetry, and for ever develops new and wonderful applications of the eternal truth which it contains. Hence epitomes have been called the moths of just history; [35] they eat out the poetry of it. The story of particular facts is as a mirror which obscures and distorts that which should be beautiful: Poetry is a mirror which makes beautiful that which is distorted.

The parts of a composition may be poetical, without the composition as a whole being a poem.[36] A single sentence

[33] 1840, 1845, Forman: no other connection.

[34] This is the comparison of history and poetry which Aristotle makes in the *Poetics:* "Poetry, therefore, is a more philosophical and a higher thing than history" (IX). Sidney makes the same argument, citing Aristotle, as does Wordsworth: "Aristotle, I have been told, has said, that Poetry is the most philosophic of all writing: it is so: its object is truth, not individual and local, but general, and operative" ("Preface," *Works*, p. 737).

[35] Shelley is probably thinking of Sir Francis Bacon's remark, "As for the corruptions and moths of history, which are epitomes, the use of them deserveth to be banished" (*Advancement of Learning*, II, ii, 4; cited by A. S. Cook in his edition of *A Defense of Poetry*, [New York, 1890]).

[36] Coleridge looked at the other side of the coin: "a poem of any length neither can be, or ought to be, all poetry" (*Biographia Literaria*, Chap XIV). Cf. Edgar Allen Poe: "a poem is such, only inasmuch as it intensely excites, by elevating, the soul; and all intense excitements are, through a physical necessity, brief. For this reason, at least one half of the 'Paradise Lost' is essentially prose" ("The Philosophy of Composition").

may be considered as a whole, though it be found in a series [37] of unassimilated portions; a single word even may be a spark of inextinguishable thought. And thus all the great historians, Herodotus, Plutarch, Livy, were poets; and although the plan of these writers, especially that of Livy,[38] restrained them from developing this faculty in its highest degree, they make copious and ample amends for their subjection, by filling all the interstices of their subjects with living images.[39]

Having determined what is poetry, and who are poets, let us proceed to estimate its effects upon society.[40]

Poetry is ever accompanied with pleasure: all spirits on which it falls open themselves to receive the wisdom which is mingled with its delight.[41] In the infancy of the world, neither poets themselves nor their auditors are fully aware of the excellence of poetry: for it acts in a divine and unapprehended manner, beyond and above consciousness; and it is reserved

---

[37] MS D (inserted), 1840, 1845, Forman: in the midst of a series.

[38] MS A gives examples: his description of the defeat of Asdrubal, the account of the orgies of the Roman Bacchants, his description of the vale of Tempe (Koszul, p. 74n.).

[39] This figure is curiously reminiscent of Keats's advice to Shelley to "'load every rift' of your subject with ore" (letter of August 1820).

[40] MS A begins this page: Poetry is the aloe which blooms once in every age, with blossoms which are ever lovely (Koszul, p. 75n.).

[41] Shelley is here developing the concept of Horace in *Ars Poetica:* "Poets wish either to profit or to delight; or to deliver at once both the pleasures and the necessaries of life." Sidney said the poet "dooth not only shew the way, but giveth so sweete a prospect into the way, as will entice anie man to enter into it" (p. 19). Wordsworth and Coleridge emphasize the pleasurable aspect of poetry: "The Poet writes under one restriction only, namely, the necessity of giving immediate pleasure to a human Being" ("Preface," *Works,* p. 737); "A poem is that species of composition, which is opposed to works of science, by proposing for its *immediate* object pleasure, not truth; and from all other species (having *this* object in common with it) it is discriminated by proposing to itself such delight from the *whole,* as is compatible with a distinct gratification from each component part" (*Biographia Literaria,* Chap. XIV).

for future generations to contemplate and measure the mighty cause and effect in all the strength and splendour of their union. Even in modern times, no living poet ever arrived at the fulness of his fame; the jury which sits in judgment upon a poet, belonging as he does to all time, must be composed of his peers: it must be impanneled by Time from the selectest of the wise of many generations.[42] A Poet is a nightingale, who sits in darkness and sings to cheer its own solitude with sweet sounds; his auditors are as men entranced by the melody of an unseen musician, who feel that they are moved and softened, yet know not whence or why.[43] The poems of Homer and his contemporaries were the delight of infant Greece; they were the elements of that social system which is the column upon which all succeeding civilization has reposed. Homer embodied the ideal perfection of his age in human character; nor can we doubt that those who read his verses were awakened to an ambition of becoming like to Achilles, Hector, and Ulysses: the truth and beauty of friendship, patriotism, and persevering devotion to an object, were unveiled to the depths in these immortal creations: the sentiments of the auditors must have been refined and enlarged by a sympathy with such great and lovely impersonations, until from admiring they imitated, and from imitation they identified themselves with the objects of their admiration. Nor let it be objected, that these characters are remote from moral perfection, and that they can by no means be considered as edifying patterns for general imitation.[44] Every epoch,

[42] A few months later (June 1821), Shelley pictured Keats as so hailed by a jury of his peers, among whom is Sidney (*Adonais*, 401).

[43] Cf. Shelley's lines in "To a Skylark":

> Like a Poet hidden
> In the hymn of thought,
> Singing hymns unbidden,
> Till the world is wrought
> To sympathy with hopes and fears it heeded not.
>
> (36–40)

[44] Cf. Sidney: "Who readeth *Aeneas* carrying old Anchises on his backe, that wisheth not it were his fortune to performe so excellent an Act?" (p. 20).

under names more or less specious, has deified its peculiar errors; Revenge is the naked Idol of the worship of a semi-barbarous age; and Self-deceit is the veiled Image of unknown evil, before which luxury and satiety lie prostrate. But a poet considers the vices of his contemporaries as the temporary dress in which his creations must be arrayed, and which cover without concealing the eternal proportions of their beauty.[45] An epic or dramatic personage is understood to wear them around his soul, as he may the antient armour or the modern uniform around his body; whilst it is easy to conceive a dress more graceful than either. The beauty of the internal nature cannot be so far concealed by its accidental vesture, but that the spirit of its form shall communicate itself to the very disguise, and indicate the shape it hides from the manner in which it is worn. A majestic form and graceful motions will express themselves through the most barbarous and tasteless costume. Few poets of the highest class have chosen to exhibit the beauty of their conceptions in its naked truth and splendour; and it is doubtful whether the alloy of costume, habit, & c., be not necessary to temper this planetary music for mortal ears.

The whole objection, however, of the immorality of poetry rests upon a misconception of the manner in which poetry acts to produce the moral improvement of man. Ethical science arranges the elements which poetry has created, and propounds schemes and proposes examples of civil and domestic life: nor is it for want of admirable doctrines that men hate, and despise, and censure, and deceive, and subjugate one another. But Poetry acts in another and diviner manner. It awakens and enlarges the mind itself by rendering the receptacle of a thousand unapprehended combinations of

---

45 This theme of a poet's adaptability is expressed in a different context in a letter to the Gisbornes on July 13, 1821: "Poets, the best of them—are a very camaelonic race: they take the colour not only of what they feed on. but the very leaves under which they pass." Cf. Keats on the "camelion Poet" in a letter of October 27, 1818 to Richard Woodhouse.

thought.[46] Poetry lifts the veil from the hidden beauty of the world,[47] and makes familiar objects be as if they were not familiar; it reproduces all that it represents, and the impersonations clothed in its Elysian light stand thenceforward in the minds of those who have once contemplated them, as memorials of that gentle and exalted content which extends itself over all thoughts and actions with which it coexists. The great secret of morals is love; or a going out of our own nature, and an identification of ourselves with the beautiful which exists in thought, action, or person, not our own.[48] A man, to be greatly good, must imagine intensely and comprehensively; he must put himself in the place of another and of many others; the pains and pleasures of his species must become his own. The great instrument of moral good is the imagination; and poetry administers to the effect by acting upon the cause.[49] Poetry enlarges the circumference of the

[46] Shelley took essentially this position in the Preface to *Prometheus Unbound* (1819): "Didactic poetry is my abhorence; nothing can be equally well expressed in prose that is not tedious and supererogatory in verse. My purpose has hitherto been simply to familiarise the highly refined imagination of the more select classes of poetical readers with beautiful idealisms of moral excellence; aware that until the mind can love, and admire, and trust, and hope, and endure, reasoned principles of moral conduct are seeds cast upon the highway of life which the unconscious passenger tramples into dust, although they bear the harvest of his happiness." Earlier Shelley had been frankly didactic: he wrote Elizabeth Hitchener on June 5, 1811, that he thought "all poetical beauty ought to be subordinate to the inculcated moral." In the Dedication to *The Cenci* (1819) he told Leigh Hunt, "I lay aside the presumptious attitude of an instructor." See *Queen Mab* and *The Revolt of Islam*.

[47] This veil imagery is Platonic, and Shelley—like Sidney—was using Plato of *The Symposium*, *The Ion*, and *The Phaedrus* to refute Plato's attack on poetry in *The Republic*. For a detailed analysis of the Platonic elements in Shelley's "Defence," see James A. Notopoulos, *The Platonism of Shelley* (Durham, N. C., 1949), pp. 346–356.

[48] See Introduction. Shelley's doctrine here is related to Plato's myth of the original four-footed, four-armed creature who was divided by the gods and ever seeks to be reunited (*The Symposium* 190).

[49] In the Preface to *The Cenci* Shelley writes: "Imagination is as the immortal God which should assume flesh for the redemption of mortal passion."

imagination by replenishing it with thoughts of ever new delight, which have the power of attracting and assimilating to their own nature all other thoughts, and which form new intervals and interstices whose void for ever craves fresh food. Poetry strengthens that faculty which is the organ of the moral nature of man, in the same manner as exercise strengthens a limb. A Poet therefore would do ill to embody his own conceptions of right and wrong, which are usually those of his place and time, in his poetical creations, which participate in neither.[50] By this assumption of the inferior office of interpreting the effect, in which perhaps after all he might acquit himself but imperfectly, he would resign the glory in a participation in the cause. There was little danger that Homer, or any of the eternal Poets, should have so far misunderstood themselves as to have abdicated this throne of their widest dominion. Those in whom the poetical faculty, though great, is less intense, as Euripides, Lucan, Tasso, Spenser, have frequently affected a moral aim, and the effect of their poetry is diminished in exact proportion to the degree in which they compel us to advert to this purpose.

Homer and the cyclic poets were followed at a certain interval by the dramatic and lyrical Poets of Athens, who flourished contemporaneously with all that is most perfect in the kindred expressions of the poetical faculty; architecture, painting, music, the dance, sculpture, philosophy, and we may add, the forms of civil life. For although the scheme of Athenian society was deformed by many imperfections which the poetry existing in Chivalry and Christianity have erased from the habits and institutions of modern Europe;

[50] Shelley had not himself always practiced this gospel, for many of his poems certainly "embody his own conceptions of right and wrong." He says in the Preface to *The Revolt of Islam:* "I have sought to enlist the harmony of metrical language, the ethereal combinations of the fancy, the rapid and subtle transitions of human passion, all those elements which essentially compose a Poem, in the cause of a liberal and comprehensive morality; and in the view of kindling within the bosoms of my readers a virtuous enthusiasm for those doctrines of liberty and justice, that faith and hope in something good which neither violence nor misrepresentation nor prejudice can ever totally extinguish among mankind."

yet never at any other period has so much energy, beauty, and virtue, been developed; [51] never was blind strength and stubborn form so disciplined and rendered subject to the will of man, or that will less repugnant to the dictates of the beautiful and the true, as during the century which preceded the death of Socrates. Of no other epoch in the history of our species have we records and fragments stamped so visibly with the image of the divinity in man.[52] But it is Poetry alone, in form, in action, or in language, which has rendered this epoch memorable above all others, and the storehouse of examples to everlasting time. For written poetry existed at that epoch simultaneously with the other arts, and it is an idle enquiry to demand which gave and which received the light, which all, as from a common focus, have scattered over the darkest periods of succeeding age.[53]

[51] MS A adds: never was such joy of life felt so intensely; never were so many individuals so free to speak or think or feel as the spirit within them dictated (Koszul, p. 79n.).

[52] MS A expands rapturously: It is as if the continent of Paradise were overwhelmed and some shattered crag remained covered with asphodel [and] amaranth which bear a golden flower (Koszul, p. 79n.). Cf. "Ode to Liberty," stanza v; and "Prologue to Hellas":

> . . . on which fell
> The dews of thought in the world's golden dawn
> Earliest and most beneign, and from it sprung
> Temples and cities and immortal forms
> And harmonies of wisdom and of song,
> And thoughts, and deeds worthy of thoughts so fair.

(32–37)

In the Preface to *Hellas* Shelley describes the ancient Greeks as "glorious beings whom the imagination almost refuses to figure to itself as belonging to our kind."

[53] In "A Discourse on the Manners of the Antient Greeks Relative to the Subject of Love" Shelley similarly discusses the general high level of Greek art, holding that "all the inventive arts maintain, as it were, a sympathetic connexion between each other, being no more than various expressions of one internal power," but suggests that Greek "poetry seems to maintain a very high, though not so disproportionate a rank, in the comparison," for Shakespeare is the "greatest individual mind, of which we have specimens remaining," and Dante perhaps "created imaginations of greater loveliness and energy" than any found in Greek literature, and

We know no more of cause and effect than a constant con-
junction of events: Poetry is ever found to coexist with what-
ever other arts contribute to the happiness and perfection of
man. I appeal to what has already been established to dis-
tinguish between the cause and the effect.

It was at the period here adverted to, that the Drama had
its birth; and however a succeeding writer may have equalled
or surpassed those few great specimens of the Athenian
drama which have been preserved to us, it is indisputable that
the art itself never was understood or practised according
to the true philosophy of it, as at Athens. For the Athen-
ians employed language, action, music, painting, the dance,
and religious institutions, to produce a common effect in
the representation of the loftiest idealisms of passion and
of power; each division in the art was made perfect in its
kind by artists of the most consummate skill, and was dis-
ciplined into a beautiful proportion and unity one towards
another. On the modern stage a few only of the elements
capable of expressing the image of the poet's conception
are employed at once. We have tragedy without music and
dancing; and music and dancing without the high imper-
sonations of which they are the fit accompaniment, and both
without religion and solemnity; religious institution has in-
deed been usually banished from the stage. Our system of
divesting the actor's face of a mask, on which the many
expressions appropriated to his dramatic character might be
moulded into one permanent and unchanging expression,
is favourable only to a partial and inharmonious effect;
it is fit for nothing but a monologue, where all the attention
may be directed to some great master of ideal mimicry. The
modern practice of blending comedy with tragedy, though

perhaps the fragments of Greek lyrics do not rival "the sublime and
chivalric sensibility of Petrarch." He still declares that "Homer must be
acknowledged to excel Shakespeare in the truth, the harmony, the
sustained grandeur, the satisfying completeness of his images, their exact
fitness to the illustration" (*Plato's Banquet*, ed. Roger Ingpen [London,
1931], pp. 4–5). For a less favorable youthful view of classical writers see
Shelley's letter of July 29, 1812 to William Godwin.

liable to great abuse in point of practice, is undoubtedly an extension of the dramatic circle; but the comedy should be as in King Lear, universal, ideal, and sublime. It is perhaps the intervention of this principle which determines the balance in favour of King Lear against the Oedipus Tyrannus or the Agamemnon, or, if you will the trilogies with which they are connected; unless the intense power of the choral poetry, especially that of the latter, should be considered as restoring the equilibrium. King Lear, if it can sustain this comparison, may be judged to be the most perfect specimen of the dramatic art existing in the world; in spite of the narrow conditions to which the poet was subjected by the ignorance of the philosophy of the drama which has prevailed in modern Europe. Calderon, in his religious Autos, has attempted to fulfil some of the high conditions of dramatic representation neglected by Shakspeare; such as the establishing a relation between the drama and religion, and the accommodating them to music and dancing; but he omits the observation of conditions still more important, and more is lost than gained by a substitution of the rigidly-defined and ever-repeated idealisms of a distorted superstition for the living impersonations of the truth of human passion.[54]

But we [55] disgress.—The Author of the Four Ages of Poetry

[54] Shelley's view of Pedro Calderón de la Barca (1600–1681) was often higher than this passage might suggest. He wrote Peacock on August 24, 1819, that he was reading Calderón in Spanish and was considering translating him, and by September 21 he could tell Peacock that he had read about a dozen of Calderón's plays and thought they deserved "to be ranked among the grandest & most perfect productions of the human mind." He reported to Leigh Hunt (November 14–18, 1819) his inexpressible wonder and delight" with the "ideal dramas of Calderon," and on November 8, 1820, he again wrote Peacock, "Plato and Calderon are my gods." Later the same month in a letter to John Gisborne he said, "I am bathing myself in the light & odour of the flowery & starry Autos," and in the spring of 1822 he translated part of Calderón's El Magico Prodigioso. See also "Letter to Maria Gisborne," 180–182.

[55] 1840, 1845, Forman: I.

has prudently omitted to dispute on the effect of the Drama upon life and manners. For, if I know the Knight by the device of his shield, I have only to inscribe Philoctetes or Agamemnon or Othello upon mine to put to flight the giant sophisms which have enchanted him, as the mirror of intolerable light though on the arm of one of the weakest of the Paladines could blind and scatter whole armies of necromancers and pagans.[56] The connexion of scenic exhibitions with the improvement or corruption of the manners of men, has been universally recognised: in other words, the presence or absence of poetry in its most perfect and universal form, has been found to be connected with good and evil in conduct and [57] habit. The corruption which has been imputed to the drama as an effect, begins, when the poetry employed in its constitution ends: I appeal to the history of manners whether the gradations [58] of the growth of the one and the decline of the other have not corresponded with an exactness equal to any other example of moral cause and effect.

The drama at Athens, or wheresoever else it may have approached to its perfection, coexisted [59] with the moral and intellectual greatness of the age. The tragedies of the Athenian poets are as mirrors in which the spectator beholds himself, under a thin disguise of circumstance, stript of all but that ideal perfection and energy which every one feels to be the internal type of all that he loves, admires, and would become. The imagination is enlarged by a sympathy with pains and passions so mighty, that they distend in their conception the capacity of that by which they are conceived; the good affections are strengthened by pity, indignation, terror and sorrow; and an exalted calm is prolonged from

[56] The passage from "The Author of the Four Ages of Poetry" through "necromancers and pagans" is canceled in darker ink in MS D and omitted in the editions.

[57] MS D, 1840, 1845, Forman: or.

[58] MS D: *word left out;* 1840, 1845, Forman: periods; MS F: the quick growth.

[59] MS D, 1840, 1845, Forman: ever co-existed.

the satiety of this high exercise of them into the tumult of familiar life: [60] even crime is disarmed of half its horror and all its contagion by being represented as the fatal consequence of the unfathomable agencies of nature; error is thus divested of its wilfulness; men can no longer cherish it as the creation of their choice. In a drama of the highest order there is little food for censure or hatred; it teaches rather self-knowledge and self-respect. Neither the eye nor the mind can see itself, unless reflected upon that which it resembles. The drama, so long as it continues to express poetry, is as a prismatic and many-sided mirror, which collects the brightest rays of human nature and divides and reproduces them from the simplicity of these elementary forms, and touches them with majesty and beauty, and multiplies all that it reflects, and endows it with the power of propagating its like wherever it may fall.[61]

But in periods of the decay of social life, the drama sympathises with that decay. Tragedy becomes a cold imitation of the form of the great masterpieces of antiquity, divested of all harmonious accompaniment of the kindred arts; and often the very form misunderstood, or a weak attempt to teach certain doctrines, which the writer considers

[60] Shelley is undoubtedly reflecting Aristotle's famous definition of tragedy (*Poetics VI*): "Tragedy then, is an imitation of an action that is serious, complete, and of a certain magnitude; in language embellished with each kind of artistic ornament, the several kinds being found in separate parts of the play; in the form of action, not of narrative; through pity and fear affecting the proper purgation of these emotions" (S. H. Butcher's translation).

[61] The best known example of this much-used figure is Hamlet's advice to the players: "the purpose of playing, whose end both at the first, and now, was and is, to hold as 'twere the mirror up to nature" (*Hamlet,* III, ii, 22–24). It goes back to Plato's *Republic:* "Do you not see that there is a way in which you could make them all yourself? . . . none quicker than that of turning a mirror round and round—you would soon enough make the sun and the heavens, and the earth and yourself, and other animals and plants, and all the other things of which we were just now speaking, in the mirror" (X. 596, Benjamin Jowett's translation). See M. H. Abrams, *The Mirror and the Lamp* (New York, 1953).

as moral truths; and which are usually no more than spe-
cious flatteries of some gross vice or weakness, with which
the author, in common with his auditors, are infected.
Hence what has been called the classical and domestic
drama. Addison's "Cato" [62] is a specimen of the one; and
would it were not superfluous to cite examples of the other!
To such purposes poetry cannot be made subservient. Poetry
is a sword of lightning, ever unsheathed, which consumes the
scabbard that would contain it. And thus we observe that all
dramatic writings of this nature are unimaginative in a
singular degree; they affect sentiment and passion, which,
divested of imagination, are other names for caprice and
appetite. The period in our own history of the grossest deg-
radation of the drama is the reign of Charles II., when
all forms in which poetry had been accustomed to be ex-
pressed became hymns to the triumph of kingly power over
liberty and virtue. Milton stood alone illuminating an age
unworthy of him.[63] At such periods the calculating principle
pervades all the forms of dramatic exhibition, and poetry
ceases to be expressed upon them. Comedy loses [64] its ideal
universality: wit succeeds to humour; we laugh from self
complacency and triumph, instead of pleasure; malignity,
sarcasm and contempt, succeed to sympathetic merriment;
we hardly laugh, but we smile.[65] Obscenity, which is ever

---

[62] *Cato*, a neoclassical tragedy by Joseph Addison, produced in 1713,
[63] Cf. *Adonais*, 29–34:

> . . . He died,
> Who was the Sire of an immortal strain,
> Blind, old, and lonely, when his country's pride,
> The priest, the slave, and the liberticide,
> Trampled and mocked with many a loathèd rite
> Of lust and blood.

[64] 1840: loves.

[65] Peacock tells of taking Shelley to see a production of Sheridan's
School for Scandal: "Shelley said to me—'I see the purpose of this comedy.
It is to associate virtue with bottles and glasses, and villany with books.'
I had great difficulty to make him stay to the end. He often talked
of 'the withering and perverting spirit of comedy.' I do not think he
ever went to another." Peacock also reports that Shelley condemned a

blasphemy against the divine beauty in life, becomes, from the very veil which it assumes, more active if less disgusting: it is a monster for which the corruption of society for ever brings forth new food, which it devours in secret.

The drama being that form under which a greater number of modes of expression of poetry are susceptible of being combined than any other, the connexion of poetry and social good is more observable in the drama than in whatever other form. And it is indisputable that the highest perfection of human society has ever corresponded with the highest dramatic excellence; and that the corruption or the extinction of the drama in a nation where it has once flourished, is a mark of a corruption of manners, and an extinction of the energies which sustain the soul of social life. But, as Machiavelli [66] says of political institutions, that life may be preserved and renewed, if men should arise capable of bringing back the drama to its principles. And this is true with respect to poetry in its most extended sense; all language institution and form, require not only to be produced but to be sustained: the office and character of a poet participates in the divine nature as regards providence, no less than as regards creation.

Civil war, the spoils of Asia, and the fatal predominance first of the Macedonian, and then of the Roman arms, were so many symbols of the extinction or suspension of the creative faculty in Greece. The bucolic writers, who found patronage under the lettered tyrants of Sicily and Egypt,

---

passage in Beaumont and Fletcher's *Rule a Wife and Have a Wife* (III, ii) as "comedy in its perfection. Society grinds down poor wretches into the dust of abject poverty, till they are scarcely recognizable as human beings; and then, instead of being treated as what they really are, subjects of the deepest pity, they are brought forward as grotesque monstrosities to be laughed at" (*Peacock's Memoirs of Shelley*, ed. H. F. B. Brett-Smith [London, 1909], p. 39–41).

[66] Probably Shelley refers to the doctrine of Niccolò Machiavelli's *The Prince* (1513) that the strong individual preserves himself by having the flexibility to adapt to fortune.

were the latest representatives of its most glorious reign.[67] Their poetry is intensely melodious; like the odour of the tuberose, it overcomes and sickens the spirit with excess of sweetness; whilst the poetry of the preceding age was as a meadow-gale of June, which mingles the fragrance of all the flowers of the field, and adds a quickening and harmonising spirit of its own which endows the sense with a power of sustaining its extreme delight. The bucolic and erotic delicacy in written poetry is correlative with that softness in statuary, music, and the kindred arts, and even in manners and institutions, which distinguished the epoch to which we [68] now refer. Nor is it the poetical faculty itself, or any misapplication of it, to which this want of harmony is to be imputed. An equal sensibility to the influence of the senses and the affections is to be found in the writings of Homer and Sophocles: the former, especially, has clothed sensual and pathetic images with irresistible attractions. Their superiority over these succeeding writers consists in the presence of those thoughts which belong to the inner faculties of our nature, not in the absence of those which are connected with the external: their incomparable perfection consists in an harmony of the union of all. It is not what the erotic writers have, but what they have not, in which their imperfection consists. It is not inasmuch as they were Poets, but inasmuch as they were not Poets, that they can be considered with any plausibility as connected with the corruption of their age. Had that corruption availed so as to extinguish in them the sensibility to pleasure, passion, and natural scenery, which is imputed to them as an imperfection, the last triumph of evil would have been achieved. For the end of social corruption is to destroy all sensibility

[67] Shelley is probably referring to Theocritus, Bion, and Moschus, elegiac poets who flourished from the third to the first centuries B.C. Shelley translated fragments from Bion and Moschus and drew upon this elegiac tradition in his *Adonais*.

[68] 1840, 1845, Forman: I.

to pleasure; and, therefore, it is corruption.[69] It begins at the imagination and the intellect as at the core, and distributes itself thence as a paralysing venom, through the affections into the very appetites, till all become a torpid mass in which sense hardly survives. At the approach of such a period, Poetry ever addresses itself to those faculties which are the last to be destroyed, and its voice is heard, like the footsteps of Astraea, departing from the world.[70] Poetry ever communicates all the pleasure which men are capable of receiving: it is ever still the light of life; the source of whatever of beautiful or generous or true can have place in an evil time. It will readily be confessed that those among the luxurious citizens of Syracuse and Alexandria, who were delighted with the poems of Theocritus, were less cold, cruel, and sensual than the remnant of their tribe. But corruption must have utterly destroyed the fabric of human society before poetry can ever cease. The sacred links of that chain have never been entirely disjoined, which descending through the minds of many men is attached to those great minds, whence as from a magnet the invisible effluence is sent forth, which at once connects, animates and sustains the life of all.[71] It is the faculty which contains within itself the seeds at once of its own and of social renovation. And let us not circumscribe the effects of the bucolic and erotic poetry within the limits of the sensibility of those

[69] MS A, at the top of the page, canceled: There is nothing in itself vicious or wrong in sensual pleasure, or unworthy in passions; so that they be not (Koszul, p. 88n.).

[70] Astraea, daughter of Zeus and Themis, was goddess of justice. She lived on the earth during the Age of Gold, was an occasional visitor in the Age of Silver, but in the Age of Brass fled to the skies, where she stands as the constellation of Virgo.

[71] A note at the bottom of the page in MS A declares: This is the language of Plato (Koszul, p. 88n.). In the same manuscript is a fragment of Shelley's translation from The Ion: For a divine power moves you, as that of the magnet; which not only can draw iron rings to itself but can endow them with a similar power of attraction to draw other rings, until a long chain of rings is attached to each other; and all is attached to the stone itself. (Koszul, p. 121).

to whom it was addressed. They may have perceived the beauty of those immortal compositions, simply as fragments and isolated portions: those who are more finely organised, or born in a happier age, may recognise them as episodes to that great poem, which all poets, like the co-operating thoughts of one great mind, have built up since the beginning of the world.[72]

The same revolutions within a narrower sphere had place in antient Rome; but the actions and forms of its social life never seem to have been perfectly saturated with the poetical element. The Romans appear to have considered the Greeks as the selectest treasuries of the selectest forms of manners and of nature, and to have abstained from creating in measured language, sculpture, music, or architecture, any thing which might bear a particular relation to their own condition, whilst it might[73] bear a general one to the universal constitution of the world. But we judge from partial evidence, and we judge perhaps partially. Ennius, Varro, Pacuvius, and Accius, all great poets, have been lost. Lucretius is in the highest, and Virgil in a very high sense, a creator. The chosen delicacy of the expressions of the latter, are as a mist of light which conceal from us the intense and exceeding truth of his conceptions of nature. Livy is instinct with poetry. Yet[74] Horace, Catullus, Ovid, and generally the other great writers of the Virgilian age,[75] saw man and nature in the mirror of Greece. The institutions also, and the religion of Rome, were less poetical than those of Greece, as the shadow is less vivid than the substance. Hence poetry in Rome, seemed to follow, rather than accompany, the perfection of political and

---

[72] The passage from "And let us not circumscribe" to "beginning of the world" is not in MS B, but an insertion is marked at its place. In MS A the passage is out of place.

[73] MS D, 1840, 1845, Forman: should.

[74] MS B lacks "Yet."

[75] Lucretius, Virgil, Horace, Catullus, and Ovid are all Roman poets of the first century B.C.

domestic society. The true poetry of Rome lived in its institutions; [76] for whatever of beautiful, true, and majestic, they contained, could have sprung only from the faculty which creates the order in which they consist. The life of Camillus,[77] the death of Regulus; [78] the expectation of the Senators, in their godlike state, of the victorious Gauls; the refusal of the Republic to make peace with Hannibal, after the battle of Cannae, were not the consequences of a refined calculation of the probable personal advantage to result from such a rhythm and order in the shews of life, to those who were at once the poets and the actors of these immortal dramas. The imagination beholding the beauty of this order, created it out of itself according to its own idea; the consequence was empire, and the reward ever-living fame. These things are not the less poetry, *quia carent vate sacro*.[79] They are the episodes of the cyclic poem written by Time upon the memories of men. The Past, like an inspired rhapsodist, fills the theatre of everlasting generations with their harmony.

[76] MS A: Yet Poetry lived & lived in Rome, contemporaneously with all the other arts which add beauty & divinity to the condition of man; except that of civil institution. But the beauty & the excellence of that system of civil society which terminated in the overthrow of the liberties of the world and of its own; and which is even now the basis of those systems of tyranny to which its barbarian destroyers have conformed, can scarcely be produced in competition with Poetry the source of whatever beauty or excellence of which any [form] or institution or opinion is susceptible. But I blaspheme. (*At the top of the page*): It is like one watching a beloved friend in pain or in decay, who murmurs half articulate consolations; which are rather felt than heard (Koszul, pp. 90*n.*, 89*n.*).

[77] Marcus Furius Camillus, famous defender of Rome from the Gauls in the fourth century B.C.

[78] Marcus Atilius Regulus, third-century B.C. Roman general who was captured by the Carthaginians and sent on parole to Rome to negotiate a peace; instead he advised the Romans to continue the war and was supposedly tortured to death on his return to Carthage.

[79] "Because they lack a sacred poet"—misquoted from Horace, *Odes* IV. 9. 28: *carent quia vate sacro*.

At length the antient system of religion and manners had fulfilled the circle of its revolution.[80] And the world would have fallen into utter anarchy and darkness, but that there were found poets among the authors of the Christian and Chivalric systems of manners and religion, who created forms of opinion and action never before conceived; which, copied into the imaginations of men, became as generals to the bewildered armies of their thoughts. It is foreign to the present purpose to touch upon the evil produced by these systems: [81] except that we protest, on the ground of the principles already established, that no portion of it can be imputed [82] to the poetry they contain.

It is probable that the astonishing [83] poetry of Moses, Job, David, Solomon, and Isaiah, had produced a great effect upon the mind of Jesus and his disciples. The scattered fragments preserved to us by the biographers of this extraordinary person, are all instinct with the most vivid poetry. But his doctrines seem to have been quickly distorted.[84]

80 1840, Forman: evolutions; MS D, 1845: revolutions.

81 In his fragmentary "Essay on the Revival of Literature" Shelley declares, "To the mind both humane and philosophical there cannot exist a greater subject of grief than the reflection of how much superstition has retarded the progress of intellect and consequently the happiness of man" (Shelley's Prose, ed. Clark, p. 179).

82 MS D, 1840, 1845, Forman: attributed.

83 Only MS B inserts "astonishing."

84 Shelley declared in a letter of May 1811, "I was once an enthusiastic Deist, but never a Christian" (Letters, I, 89). He believed, as he said in his notes to Queen Mab (1813) in "a pervading Spirit coeternal with the universe," but not in the divinity of Jesus: "It is impossible to believe that the Spirit that pervades this infinite machine begat a son upon the body of a Jewish woman." He admired Jesus, as "a man of pure life, who desired to rescue his countrymen from the tyranny of their barbarous and degrading superstitions" (Works, ed. Thomas Hutchinson [Oxford Standard Edition], pp. 812, 801, 820), but thought as he puts it in "A Philosophical View of Reform" (1820), "Names borrowed from the life and opinions of Jesus Christ were employed as symbols of domination and imposture, and a system of liberty and equality (for such was the system preached by that great Reformer) was perverted to support

At a certain period after the prevalence of doctrines [85] founded upon those promulgated by him, the three forms into which Plato had distributed the faculties of mind underwent a sort of apotheosis, and became the object of the worship of Europe.[86] Here it is to be confessed that "Light seems to thicken," and

> The crow makes wing to the rooky wood,
> Good things of day begin to droop and drowse,
> And night's black agents to their preys do rouse.[87]

But mark how beautiful an order has sprung from the dust and blood of this fierce chaos! how the World, as from a

---

oppression" (*Shelley's Prose*, p. 230). In *Prometheus Unbound* he thus describes Christ and the distortion of his doctrines:

> One came forth of gentle worth
> Smiling on the sanguine earth;
> His words outlived him, like swift poison
> Withering up truth, peace, and pity.
> Look! where round the wide horizon
> Many a million-peopled city
> Vomits smoke in the bright air.
> Hark that outcry of despair!
> 'Tis his mild and gentle ghost
> Wailing for the faith he kindled.
> (I, 546–555)

see also "Essay on Christianity" (*Shelley's Prose*, p. 198).

[85] MS D, 1840, 1845, Forman: a system of opinions.

[86] MS D, 1840, 1845, Forman: of the civilised world. Cf. Plato, *Republic* 435ff.; and *Timaeus* 89: "As I have often said, that there are three kinds of soul, located within us, each of them having their own proper motions— so I must now say in the fewest words possible, that the one part, if remaining inactive and ceasing from the natural motion, must necessarily become very weak, but when trained and exercised then very strong" (Jowett's translation). Plato's point here is that a harmony should be established among the souls; but he gives the primacy to the "divine power" in the brain, over the intermediate, mortal soul seated in the heart, and the lower sensuous soul of the body. Probably Shelley means the "apotheosis" of the rational.

[87] 1840: so roude. The passage is slightly misquoted from *Macbeth*, III, ii, 50–53. Shelley is probably echoing Peacock's ironic remark about the darkness which spread with the light of the Gospel.

resurrection, balancing itself on the golden wings of knowledge and of hope, has reassumed its yet unwearied flight into the Heaven of time. Listen to the music, unheard by outward ears, which is as a ceaseless and invisible wind, nourishing its everlasting course with strength and swiftness.[88]

The poetry in the doctrines of Jesus Christ, and the mythology and institutions of the Celtic [89] conquerors of the Roman empire, outlived the darkness and the convulsions connected with their growth and victory, and blended themselves into a new fabric of manners and opinion. It is an error to impute the ignorance of the dark ages to the Christian doctrines or the predominance of the Celtic nations. Whatever of evil their agencies may have contained sprang from the extinction of the poetical principle, connected with the progress of despotism and superstition. Men, from causes too intricate to be here discussed, had become insensible and selfish: their own will had become feeble, and yet they were its slaves, and thence the slaves of the will of others: lust, fear, avarice, cruelty, and fraud, characterised a race amongst whom no one was to be found capable of *creating* in form, language, or institution. The moral anomalies of such a state of society are not justly to be charged upon any class of events immediately connected with them, and those events are most entitled to our approbation which could dissolve it most expeditiously. It is unfortunate for those who cannot distinguish words from thoughts, that many of these anomalies have been incorporated into our popular religion.[90]

88 In his draft Shelley criticizes this passage: "But this is not argument—not illustration—an illustration ought not to precede the thing to be illustrated." (Koszul, p. 92n.).

89 Shelley apparently used Celtic to mean Germanic.

90 MS A: thus when speaking popularly [we impute] to Christianity the absurdity, [the bloodshed, the persecutions] and iniquitous effects which have rendered the name almost infamous, we mean, according to a philosophical interpretation that such are the consequences of the extinction of the poetical faculty (Koszul, pp. 93–94n.).

It was not until the eleventh century that the effects of the poetry of the Christian and Chivalric systems began to manifest themselves. The principle of equality had been discovered and applied by Plato in his Republic, as the theoretical rule of the mode in which the materials of pleasure and of power produced by the common skill and labour of human beings ought to be distributed among them. The limitations of this rule were asserted by him to be determined only by the sensibility of each, or the utility to result to all.[91] Plato, following the doctrines of Timaeus and Pythagoras, taught also a moral and intellectual system of doctrine, comprehending at once the past, the present, and the future condition of man.[92] Jesus Christ divulged the sacred and eternal truths contained in these views to mankind, and Christianity, in its abstract purity, became the exoteric expression of the esoteric doctrines of the poetry and wisdom of antiquity. The incorporation of the Celtic nations with the exhausted population of the south, impressed upon it the figure of the poetry existing in their mythology and institutions. The result was a sum of the action and reaction of all the causes included in it; for it may be assumed as a maxim that no nation or religion can supersede any other without incorporating into itself a portion of that which it supersedes. The abolition of personal and domestic slavery, and the emancipation

[91] This view is pervasive in Plato's *Republic*. Commentators have suggested that Shelley had in mind passages beginning at 369, 416, 464, and 543. Shelley discusses Plato's doctrine in connection with Christ's teachings in "Essay on Christianity" (*Shelley's Prose*, pp. 207–208).

[92] Cf. Shelley's amusing "Essay on the Devil and Devils": "Plato, following his master Socrates, who had been struck with the beauty and novelty of the theistical hypothesis as first delivered by the tutor of Pericles, supposed the existence of a God, and accommodated a moral system of the most universal character, including the past, the present, and the future condition of man, to the popular supposition of the moral superintendence of this one intellectual cause" (*Shelley's Prose*, p. 265).

of women from a great part of the degrading restraints of antiquity, were among the consequences of these events.

The abolition of personal slavery is the basis of the highest political hope thăt it can enter into the mind of man to conceive. The freedom of women produced the poetry of sexual love.[93] Love became a religion, the idols of whose worship were ever present. It was as if the statues of Apollo and the Muses had been endowed with life and motion, and had walked forth among their worshippers; so that earth became peopled by the inhabitants of a diviner world.[94] The familiar appearance and proceedings of life became wonderful and heavenly; and a paradise was created as out of the wrecks of Eden.[95] And as this creation itself is poetry, so its creators were poets; and language was the instrument of their art: "Galeotto fù il libro, e chi lo scrisse." [96] The Provençal Trouveurs, or inventors, preceded Petrarch, whose verses are as spells, which unseal the inmost enchanted fountains of the delight which is in the grief of love. It

[93] Of course, Shelley's second wife was Mary Godwin, the daughter of Mary Wollstonecraft, author of *Vindication of the Rights of Woman* (1792).

[94] By October 1820 Shelley had received Keats's last volume, *Lamia, Isabella, and Other Poems,* and although he thought it "insignificant enough" except for the "astonishing" fragment of *Hyperion* (letter to Peacock, November 8, 1820), he may have been influenced here by Keats's rather Byronic passage in "Lamia":

> Let the mad poets say whate'er they please
> Of the sweets of Faeries, Peris, Goddesses,
> There is not such a treat among them all,
> Haunters of cavern, lake, and waterfall,
> As a real woman, lineal indeed
> From Pyrrha's pebbles or old Adam's seed.
> (Part I, 328–333)

[95] Shelley was ever yearning for some paradise wrought by love; see, for example, *Epipsychidion,* 388 ff.

[96] "Gallehaut was the book, and he who wrote it." The quotation is not in Shelley's draft. It comes from Dante's *Divina Commedia,* the Fifth Canto of the *Inferno,* in which Francesca da Rimini explains how she was tempted to the carnal sin that condemned her to the Second Circle of Hell: she and her lover were reading of the love affair of Lancelot and Guenever, in which Gallehaut plays the go-between.

is impossible to feel them without becoming a portion of
that beauty which we contemplate: it were superfluous to
explain how the gentleness and the elevation of mind con-
nected with these sacred emotions can render men more
amiable, and generous [97] and wise, and lift them out of the
dull vapours of the little world of self.[98] Dante understood
the secret things of love even more than Petrarch. His *Vita
Nuova* is an inexhaustible fountain of purity of sentiment
and language: it is the idealised history of that period,
and those intervals of his life which were dedicated to
love. His apotheosis of Beatrice in Paradise, and the grada-
tions of his own love and her loveliness, by which as by
steps he feigns himself to have ascended to the throne of
the Supreme Cause, is the most glorious imagination of
modern poetry. The acutest critics have justly reversed the
judgment of the vulgar, and the order of the great acts
of the "Divine Drama," [99] in the measure of the admiration
which they accord to the Hell, Purgatory, and Paradise.
The latter is a perpetual hymn of everlasting Love. Love,
which found a worthy poet in Plato alone of all the an-
tients,[100] has been celebrated by a chorus of the greatest
writers of the renovated world; and the music has pene-

[97] MS D, 1840, 1845, Forman: more generous.

[98] Cf. *Adonais*, particularly the next-to-the-last stanza.

> That Light whose smile kindles the Universe,
> That Beauty in which all things work and move,
> That Benediction which the eclipsing Curse
> Of birth can quench not, that sustaining Love
> Which through the web of being blindly wove
> By man and beast and earth and air and sea,
> Burns bright or dim, as each are mirrors of
> The fire for which all thirst; now beams on me,
> Consuming the last clouds of cold mortality.

[99] 1840, Forman: Divina Commedia.

[100] Shelley is probably referring to *The Symposium*, particularly to
Agathon's glowing praise of the god of love. A piece of this, in Shelley's
1818 translation, goes: "Love seems to me, O Phaedrus, a divinity the
most beautiful and the best of all, and the author to all others of the
excellences with which his own nature is endowed" (*Plato's Banquet*, ed.
Ingpen, p. 67).

trated the caverns of society, and its echoes still drown the
dissonance of arms and superstition. At successive inter-
vals, Ariosto, Tasso, Shakspeare, Spenser, Calderon, Rous-
seau,[101] and the great writers of our own age, have celebrated
the dominion of love,[102] planting as it were trophies in the
human mind of that sublimest victory over sensuality and
force. The true relation borne to each other by the sexes
into which human kind is distributed, has become less mis-
understood; and if the error which confounded diversity
with inequality of the powers of the two sexes has become [103]
partially recognised in the opinions and institutions of mod-
ern Europe, we owe this great benefit to the worship of
which Chivalry was the law, and poets the prophets.

The poetry of Dante may be considered as the bridge
thrown over the stream of time, which unites the modern
and antient World.[104] The distorted notions of invisible
things which Dante and his rival Milton have idealised,
are merely the mask and the mantle in which these great
poets walk through eternity enveloped and disguised. It is
a difficult question to determine how far they were con-
scious of the distinction which must have subsisted in their
minds between their own creeds and that of the people.
Dante at least appears to wish to mark the full extent of
it by placing Riphaeus, whom Virgil calls *justissimus unus*,[105]
in Paradise, and observing a most heretical [106] caprice in his
distribution of rewards and punishments. And Milton's

[101] Shelley's unfinished last poem, "The Triumph of Life," presents
Rousseau as a grotesque narrator who declares, "I was overcome/ By my
own heart alone" (240–241).

[102] MS A: sexual love.

[103] MS D, 1840, 1845: been.

[104] MS A: Let us refrain from a discussion [of] the origin of those
monstrous opinions which Dante & Milton idealized which involves no
less than an inquiry into the origin of evil (Koszul, p. 97n.).

[105] "The one justest man" (*Aeneid* II. 426–427). Dante places the Trojan
Riphaeus in Paradise, fifth of the holy lights in the circle of the Just,
although he died before the birth of Christ (*Paradiso*, XX).

[106] 1840: poetical.

poem contains within itself a philosophical refutation of that system, of which, by a strange and natural antithesis, it has been a chief popular support. Nothing [107] can exceed the energy and magnificence of the character of Satan as expressed in "Paradise Lost." It is a mistake to suppose that he could ever have been intended for the popular personification of evil. Implacable hate, patient cunning and a sleepless refinement of device to inflict the extremest anguish on an enemy, these things are evil; and, although venial in a slave, are not to be forgiven in a tyrant; although redeemed by much that ennobles his defeat in one subdued, are marked by all that dishonours his conquest in the victor. Milton's Devil as a moral being is as far superior to his God, as One who perseveres in some purpose which he has conceived to be excellent in spite of adversity and torture, is to One who in the cold security of undoubted triumph inflicts the most horrible revenge upon his enemy, not from any mistaken notion of inducing him to repent of a perseverance in enmity, but with the alleged design of exasperating him to deserve new torments. Milton has so far violated the popular creed (if this shall be judged to be a violation) as to have alleged no superiority of moral virtue to his God over his Devil.[108] And this bold neglect of a direct moral purpose is the most decisive proof of the supremacy of Milton's genius. He mingled as it were the elements of human nature as colours upon a single pallet, and arranged them in the composition of his great picture according to the laws of epic truth; that is, according to the laws of that principle by which a series of actions of the external universe and of intelligent and ethical beings is calculated to excite the sympathy of succeeding generations of man-

[107] The passage beginning here and ending 29 lines below with "succeeding generations of mankind" is only slightly reworked from "Essay on the Devil and Devils" (*Shelley's Prose,* p. 267).

[108] Cf. William Blake, "The reason Milton wrote in fetters when he wrote of Angels & God, and at liberty when he wrote of Devils & Hell, is because he was a true Poet and of the Devil's party without knowing it" (*The Marriage of Heaven and Hell,* "The Voice of the Devil").

kind. The Divina Commedia and Paradise Lost have con-
ferred upon modern mythology a systematic form; and
when change and time shall have added one more supersti-
tion to the mass of those which have arisen and decayed
upon the earth, commentators will be learnedly employed
in elucidating the religion of ancestral Europe, only not
utterly forgotten because it will have been stamped with
the eternity of genius.

Homer was the first and Dante the second epic poet:
that is, the second poet, the series of whose creations bore
a defined and intelligible relation to the knowledge and
sentiment and religion and political conditions [109] of the age
in which he lived, and of the ages which followed it: devel-
oping itself in correspondence with their development. For
Lucretius had limed the wings of his swift spirit in the
dregs of the sensible world; [110] and Virgil, with a modesty
which ill became his genius, had affected the fame of an
imitator, even whilst he created anew all that he copied;
and none among the flock of Mock-birds, though their notes
were sweet, Apollonius Rhodius, Quintus Calaber Smyr-
naeus, Nonnus, Lucan, Statius, or Claudian,[111] have sought

[109] MS D, 1840, 1845, Forman omit "and political conditions."

[110] MS A: Lucretius entangled the wings of his swift spirit in atoms
(Koszul, p. 99n.). Above Shelley called Lucretius "in the highest . . .
sense, a creator." Probably in this context he is thinking of the materialism
and skepticism of De rerum natura.

[111] Apollonius Rhodius, Alexandrian poet of the second century B.C.,
was the author of Argonautica. Quintus Smyrnaeus, called Calaber
because of the discovery in Calabria of the only known manuscript of
his Posthomerica, a 14-volume Greek continuation of Homer, lived in the
later part of the fourth century A.D. Nonnus, a Greek poet of the fifth
century A.D., wrote the Dionysiaca, a 48-book epic. Lucan (Marcus
Annaeus Lucanus) was a Roman poet born in Spain in the first century
A.D., best known for his Pharsalia. Publius Papinius Statius, also a Roman
poet of the first century A.D., was the author of the Thebiad. Claudian
(Claudius Claudianus) was a Roman poet probably born in Alexandria
in the fourth century A.D. who wrote an epic Rape of Proserpine.
Smyrnaeus' name has caused trouble: it is misspelled "Smyrnetheus"
in MS B. In MS D, 1840, and Forman there is a misleading comma

even to fulfil a single condition of epic truth. Milton was
the third epic poet.[112] For if the title of epic in its highest
sense be refused to the Aeneid, still less can it be conceded
to the Orlando Furioso, the Gerusalemme Liberata, the
Lusiad, or the Fairy Queen.[113]

Dante and Milton were both deeply penetrated with the
antient religion of the civilized world; and its spirit exists
in their poetry probably in the same proportion as its
forms survived in the unreformed worship of modern Eur-
ope. The one preceded and the other followed the Reforma-
tion at almost equal intervals.[114] Dante was the first religious
reformer, and Luther surpassed him rather in the rudeness
and acrimony, than in the boldness of his censures of papal
usurpation. Dante was the first awakener of entranced
Europe; he created a language, in itself music and per-
suasion, out of a chaos of inharmonious barbarisms. He was
the congregator of those great spirits who presided over
the resurrection of learning; the Lucifer [115] of that starry

---

between Calaber and Smyrnaeus, and 1845 tried to solve the problem
by leaving out "Smyrnaeus" and calling him simply Quintus Calaber.

[112] In *Adonais* Shelley calls Milton "the third among the sons of
light" (36).

[113] Ariosto's *Orlando Furioso* (1532) and Tasso's *Jerusalem Delivered*
(1576) are romantic Italian epic poems. *Os Lusiadas* (1572), by the
Portuguese poet Luis de Camoëns, celebrates the descendants of the
legendary hero, Lusus. Edmund Spenser published only six (1589–1596)
of the projected twelve books of the *Faerie Queene*. Shelley used the
Spenserian stanza in *Adonais*. He did not much like Ariosto, finding him
lacking in sensibility; Tasso, he thought, had more delicate sensibility
but was marred by artificiality. See letter to John and Maria Gisborne,
July 10, 1818.

[114] MS A continues: They have presented the mythology of the new
religion under a precise form; so that, by a definiteness of object &
purpose, the labours of those are abridged, who as pioneers of the
overgrowth of ages, devote themselves first to prune the dead branches
& then to remove the sapless & rotten trunks of an outworn forest of
opinions which towards the decay of a popular faith usurps the soil
of a new and more beautiful birth (Koszul, p. 100*n*.).

[115] Shelley is here apparently using "Lucifer" in a good sense, the
"light bearer" before he became a fallen angel.

flock which in the thirteenth century shone forth from republican Italy, as from a heaven, into the darkness of the benighted world. His very words are instinct with spirit; each is as a spark, a burning atom of inextinguishable thought; and many yet lie covered in the ashes of their birth, and pregnant with a lightning which has yet found no conductor. All high poetry is infinite; it is as the first acorn, which contained all oaks potentially. Veil after veil may be undrawn, and the inmost naked beauty of the meaning never exposed.[116] A great poem is a fountain for ever overflowing with the waters of wisdom and delight; and after one person and one age has exhausted all its divine effluence which their peculiar relations enable them to share, another and yet another succeeds, and new relations are ever developed, the source of an unforeseen and an unconceived delight.[117]

The age immediately succeeding to that of Dante, Petrarch, and Boccaccio, was characterized by a revival of painting, sculpture, music,[118] and architecture. Chaucer caught the sacred inspiration, and the superstructure of English literature is based upon the materials of Italian invention.[119]

But let us not be betrayed from a defence into a critical history of Poetry and its influence on Society. Be it enough to have pointed out the effects of poets,[120] in the large and

[116] MS A adds: After one person or one age has exhausted all the divinity which its peculiar relations with them enable it to draw forth, another and yet another succeeds & finds new relations develop which forever produce new pleasure and knowledge. [Canceled: They are as] A great Poem is torches from which a thousand lamps may be enkindled (Koszul, pp. 100–101n.).

[117] MS B, a canceled passage continues: Poetry is as [the] a star whose light is so intense and whose height is so immeasurably great, that distance . . . at the most distant extremes of the orbit of the earth (Julian, VII, 356).

[118] 1840, 1845, Forman omit "music."

[119] Sidney had written: "So in the Italian language, the first that made it aspire to be a treasure-house of Science, were the Poets Dante, Bocace, and Petrarch. So in our English wer Gower and Chawcer" (p. 4).

[120] Ms B: poetry.

true sense of the word, upon their own and all succeeding times, and to revert [121] to the partial instances cited as illustrations of an opinion the reverse of that attempted to be established by the Author of the Four Ages of Poetry.

But poets have been challenged to resign the civic crown to reasoners and mechanists on another plea. It is admitted that the exercise of the imagination is most delightful, but it is alleged, that that of reason is more useful. Let us examine as the grounds of this distinction, what is here meant by utility. Pleasure or good, in a general sense, is that which the consciousness of a sensitive and intelligent being seeks, and in which, when found, it acquiesces. There are two modes or degrees [122] of pleasure, one durable, universal and permanent; the other transitory and particular.[123] Utility may either express the means of producing the

[121] The passage from "and to revert" to the end of the paragraph is canceled in MS D and omitted from the editions.

[122] MS D first read "two modes or signs," but corrected to "two kinds," the reading of the editions. MS A: and there are various gradations of pleasure, some more durable and intense than others (Koszul, p. 102n.).

[123] MS C:

In one sense Utility expresses the means for producing and fixing the most intense and durable and universal pleasure, and has relation to our intellectual being; in another it expresses the means of banishing the importunity of the wants of our animal nature; and surrounding us with security and tranquility of life, destroying the grosser desires, superstition, &c., and conciliating such a degree of mutual forbearance between men as may spring from motives consistent with their own present and manifest advantage.—The author of The Four Ages of Poetry employs it solely in the latter sense.

Undoubtedly the promoters of Utility, in this limited sense, have their due praise; they have their appointed office in society; they follow the footsteps of poets and copy their creations into the book of familiar life, and their exertions are of the highest value so long as they confine their administration to the concerns of the inferior powers of our nature within the limits of what is consistent with what is due to the superior ones. But whilst the sceptic destroys gross superstitions, let him not as some French writers have done, destroy the eternal truths written upon the minds and imaginations of men. Whilst the mechanist abridges, and the political economist combines labour, let them beware that the consequences of their speculations do not tend,

former or the latter. In the former sense, whatever strengthens and purifies the affections, enlarges the imagination, and adds spirit to sense, is useful. But the meaning in which the Author of the Four Ages of Poetry seems to have employed the word utility is the narrower one of banishing [124] the importunity of the wants of our animal nature, the surrounding men with security of life, the dispersing the grosser delusions of superstition, and the conciliating such a degree of mutual forbearance among men as may consist with the motives of personal advantage.

Undoubtedly the promoters of utility, in this limited sense, have their appointed office in society. They follow the footsteps of poets, and copy the sketches of their `creations into the book of common life. They make space, and give time. Their exertions are of the highest value, so long as they confine their administration of the concerns of the

---

as they have in modern England, to exasperate at once the extremes of luxury and want. But without an intermixture of the poetical element, such are the effects which must ever flow from the unmitigated exercise of the reason. The rich become richer, and the poor become poorer; and tyranny and anarchy alternately furious.

It is difficult to define pleasure in the highest sense, without combining a number of words which produce apparent paradoxes on account of the incommunicability of popular and philosophical [gap] from an inexplicable want of harmony in the constitution of our mortal being. The pain of the inferior is frequently synonymous with the pleasure of the superior portions of our nature, and terror, anguish, sorrow, despair itself, are often the selectest expressions of our approximation to this good. On this depends our pleasure with tragic fiction. Our pleasure in tragic fiction depends on this principle; and tragedy produces pleasure by affording a shadow of the pleasure which exists in intense [gap] This is the source also of the melancholy which is inseparable from the sweetest melody. The pleasure in sorrow is far intenser than that of pleasure itself, and it is sweeter to enter into the house of mourning than into the house of mirth. The pleasure of comedy is to that of tragedy as the pleasure of the senses to that of the imagination (*Works of Shelley*, ed. H. B. Forman [London, 1880], VII, 130–132n.).

124 The passage from "the meaning" to "banishing" is in MS D and uncanceled, but it is cut from the editions and replaced by: But a narrower meaning may be assigned to the word utility, confining it to express that which banishes.

inferior powers of our nature within the limits due to the superior ones. But whilst the sceptic destroys gross superstitions, let him spare to deface, as some of the French writers have defaced, the eternal truths charactered upon the imaginations of men. Whilst the mechanist abridges, and the political economist combines, labour, let them beware that their speculations, for want of correspondence with those first principles which belong to the imagination, do not tend, as they have in modern England, to exasperate at once the extremes of luxury and want. They have exemplified the saying, "To him that hath, more shall be given; and from him that hath not, the little that he hath shall be taken away." [125] The rich have become richer, and the poor have become poorer; and the vessel of the state is driven between the Scylla and Charybdis of anarchy and despotism. Such are the effects which must ever flow from an unmitigated exercise of the calculating faculty.

It is difficult to define pleasure in its highest sense; the definition involving a number of apparent paradoxes. For, from an inexplicable defect of harmony in the constitution of human nature, the pain of the inferior is frequently connected with the pleasures of the superior portions of our being. Sorrow, terror, anguish, despair itself, are often the chosen expressions of an approximation to the highest good. Our sympathy in tragic fiction depends on this principle; tragedy delights by affording a shadow of the pleasure which exists in pain. This is the source also of the melancholy which is inseparable from the sweetest melody.[126] The pleasure that is in sorrow is sweeter than the

[125] Approximate quotation from the *New Testament:* cf. Matthew 25:29, Mark 4:25, Luke 8:18, 19:26.

[126] Shelley's ideas here suggest the Graveyard School and Edmund Burke's theory that terror is the basis of the sublime (*Philosophical Enquiry into the Origin of our Ideas of the Sublime and Beautiful,* 1756). Wordsworth also declared

> I too exclusively esteemed *that* love,
> And sought *that* beauty, which, as Milton sings,
> Hath terror in it.

> (*Prelude,* XIV, 244–246)

pleasure of pleasure itself. And hence the saying, "It is bet-
ter to go to the house of mourning, than to the house
of mirth." [127] Not that this highest species of pleasure is
necessarily linked with pain. The delight of love and friend-
ship, the ecstasy of the admiration of nature, the joy of
the perception and still more of the creation of poetry is
often wholly unalloyed.

The production and assurance of pleasure in this highest
sense is true utility.[128] Those who produce and preserve this
pleasure are Poets or poetical philosophers.

The [129] exertions of Locke, Hume, Gibbon, Voltaire, Rous-
seau,[130] and their disciples, in favour of oppressed and delud-
ed humanity, are entitled to the gratitude of mankind. Yet
it is easy to calculate the degree of moral and intellectual
improvement which the world would have exhibited, had
they never lived. A little more nonsense would have been
talked for a century or two; and perhaps a few more men,
women, and children, burnt as heretics. We might not at
this moment have been congratulating each other on the

(See *Paradise Lost,* IX, 490–491: "though terrour be in Love/ and
beautie.") Cf. also "To a Skylark":

> Our sincerest laughter
> With some pain is frought;
> Our sweetest songs are those that tell
> Of saddest thought.
>
> (88–91)

127 Shelley has supplied the alliteration: Ecclesiastes 7:2 reads: "It
is better to go to the house of mourning, than to go to the house of
feasting."

128 Shelley seems to be anticipating John Stuart Mill's qualitative
modifications of the crude quantitative pleasure principle of Jeremy
Bentham and the older Utilitarians.

129 In MS B a canceled beginning of this sentence goes: No one can
regard with more reverence than I do the (*Julian,* VII, 357).

130 I follow the classification adopted by the Author of the Four Ages
of Poetry; but he was essentially a Poet. The others, even Voltaire, were
mere reasoners. [Shelley's footnote in MSS B and D, changed in editions
to read: Although Rousseau has been thus classed, he was essentially
a poet. The others, even Voltaire, were mere reasoners.]

abolition of the Inquisition in Spain.[131] But it exceeds all imagination to conceive what would have been the moral condition of the world if neither Dante, Petrarch, Boccaccio, Chaucer, Shakspeare, Calderon, Lord Bacon, nor Milton, had ever existed; if Raphael and Michael Angelo had never been born; if the Hebrew poetry had never been translated; if a revival of the study of Greek literature had never taken place; if no monuments of antient sculpture had been handed down to us; and if the poetry of the religion of the antient world had been extinguished together with its belief. The human mind could never, except by the intervention of these excitements, have been awakened to the invention of the grosser sciences, and that application of analytical reasoning to the aberrations of society, which it is now attempted to exalt over the direct expression of the inventive and creative faculty itself.[132]

We have more moral, political and historical wisdom, than we know how to reduce into practice; we have more scientific and economical knowledge than can be accommodated to the just distribution of the produce which it multiplies. The poetry in these systems of thought, is concealed by the accumulation of facts and calculating processes. There is no want of knowledge respecting what is wisest and best in morals, government, and political ecónomy, or at least, what is wiser and better than what men now practise and endure. But we let *"I dare not* wait upon *I would,* like the poor cat i' the adage." [133] We

[131] Although Napoleon has dissolved the Spanish Inquisition in 1808, after the restoration of Ferdinand VII it was reinstituted until an insurrection in 1820 forced its final abolition.

[132] MS A adds: The author of the four ages of Poetry closes his paper with an exhibition in array of all the denominations of the subordinate arts of life which are employed upon working out of the elements originally furnished by the poetical faculty, materials of knowledge and power. And he protests against an attempt to create new elements by that only process, exhorting us [at the same time to cultivate in preference] (Koszul, pp. 105–106n.).

[133] *Macbeth,* I, vii, 44–45. Forman has pointed out that Shelley liked this "adage" well enough to quote it also in *Zastrozzi* and *Proposals for*

want the creative faculty to imagine that which we know; we want the generous impulse to act that which we imagine; we want the poetry of life: our calculations have outrun conception; we have eaten more than we can digest.[134] The cultivation of those sciences which have enlarged the limits of the empire of man over the external world, has, for want of the poetical faculty, proportionally circumscribed those of the internal world; and man, having enslaved the elements, remains himself a slave. To what but a cultivation of the mechanical arts in a degree disproportioned to the presence of the creative faculty, which is the basis of all knowledge, is to be attributed the abuse of all invention for abridging and combining labour, to the exasperation of the inequality of mankind? From what other cause has it arisen that these inventions [135] which should have lightened, have added a weight to the curse imposed on Adam? [136] Thus Poetry, and the principle of Self, of which Money is the visible incarnation, are the God and Mammon of the world.

The functions of the poetical faculty are twofold; by one it creates new materials for knowledge, and power and pleasure; by the other it engenders in the mind a desire to reproduce and arrange them according to a certain rhythm and order which may be called the beautiful and the good. The cultivation of poetry is never more to be desired than at periods when, from an excess of the selfish and calculating principle, the accumulation of the materials of external life exceed the quantity of the power of assimilat-

---

an Association of Philanthropists (VII, 135n.). See also Shelley's letter of November 4, 1814, to Mary Godwin.

[134] At the top of this page in his draft Shelley wrote and canceled: Poetry is the representation of the benevolent principle in man, as [gold] [property] is the representation of the selfish principle: they are the God and the Mammon of the world (Koszul, p. 106n.).

[135] MSS A and D read "the inventions," corrected to "the discoveries," which is the reading of the editions.

[136] Genesis 3:17: "cursed is the ground for thy sake; in sorrow shalt thou eat of it all the days of thy life."

ing them to the internal laws of human nature. The body has then become too unwieldy for that which animates it.

Poetry is indeed something divine.[137] It is at once the centre and circumference of knowledge; it is that which comprehends all science, and that to which all science must be referred.[138] It is at the same time the root and blossom of all other systems of thought; it is that from which all spring, and that which adorns all; and that which, if blighted, denies the fruit and the seed, and withholds from the barren world the nourishment and the succession of the scions of the tree of life. It is the perfect and consummate surface and bloom of things;[139] it is as the odour and the colour of the rose to the texture of the elements which compose it, as the form and the splendour of unfaded beauty to the secrets of anatomy and corruption. What were Virtue, Love, Patriotism, Friendship—what were the scenery of this beautiful Universe which we inhabit; what were our consolations on this side of the grave, and what were our aspirations beyond it, if Poetry did not ascend to bring light and fire from those eternal regions where the owl-winged faculty of calculation dare not ever soar? Poetry is not like reasoning, a power to be exerted according to the determination of the will. A man cannot say, "I will compose poetry." The greatest poet even cannot say

[137] Cf. Sidney's *Apologie:* "For *Poesie* must not be drawne by the eares, it must be gently led, or rather it must lead, which is partly the cause that made the auncient learned affirme, it was a divine gift & no humane skil" (p. 37). Also Plato's *Phaedrus* 245: "There is also a third kind of madness, which is a possession of the Muses; this enters into a delicate and virgin soul, and there inspiring frenzy, awakens lyric and all other numbers . . . . But he who, not being inspired and having no touch of madness in his soul, comes to the door and thinks that he will get into the temple by the help of art—he, I say, and his poetry are not admitted" (Jowett translation).

[138] Cf. Wordsworth: "Poetry is the breath and finer spirit of all knowledge; it is the impassioned expression which is the countenance of all Science" ("Preface," *Works,* p. 738).

[139] 1840, 1845, Forman: all things.

it: for the mind in creation is as a fading coal,[140] which some invisible influence, like an inconstant wind, awakens to transitory brightness: this power arises from within, like the colour of a flower which fades and changes as it is developed, and the conscious portions of our natures are unprophetic either of its approach or its departure. Could this influence be durable in its original purity and force, it is impossible to predict the greatness of the results; but when composition begins, inspiration is already on the decline, and the most glorious poetry that has ever been communicated to the world is probably a feeble shadow of the original conception of the Poet. I appeal to the great [141] poets of the present day, whether it be not an error to assert that the finest passages of poetry are produced by labour and study.[142] The toil and the delay recommended by critics, can be justly interpreted to mean no more than a careful observation of the inspired moments, and an artificial connexion of the spaces between their suggestions by the intertexture of conventional expressions; a necessity only

140 M. T. Solve suggests that Shelley is here reflecting Plautinus' "notion of creation as a falling-away from the perfection of the ideal" (*Shelley: His Theory of Poetry* [Chicago, 1927], p. 43).

141 MS D, 1840, 1845, Forman: greatest.

142 They would have agreed in part: Keats declared that "if Poetry comes not as naturally as the Leaves to a tree it had better not come at all" (letter to John Taylor, February 27, 1818), but in another mood he said that poetry is "not so fine a thing as philosophy" (letter to George and Georgiana Keats, March 19, 1819); Wordsworth defined poetry as "the spontaneous overflow of powerful feelings" (Preface," *Works*, p. 740), but also wrote W. R. Hamilton, "the logical faculty has infinitely more to do with poetry than the young and the inexperienced, whether writer or critic, ever dreams of. Indeed, as the materials upon which that faculty is exercised in poetry are so subtle, so plastic, so complex, the application of it requires an adroitness which can proceed from nothing but practice; a discernment, which emotion is so far from bestowing that at first it is ever in the way of it" (September 24, 1827); Byron called poetry "the lava of the imagination" and declared that he could not polish; if he missed his spring he went crawling back into the jungle. Cf. Shelley's "Ode to Naples," 50–51, and the canceled fragments of the "Ode to Heaven," 5.

imposed by the limitedness of the poetical faculty itself. For Milton conceived the Paradise Lost as a whole before he executed it in portions. We have his own authority also for the Muse having "dictated" to him the "unpremeditated song," [143] and let this be an answer to those who would allege the fifty-six various readings of the first line of the Orlando Furioso. Compositions so produced are to poetry what mosaic is to painting. This instinct and intuition of the poetical faculty is still more observable in the plastic and pictorial arts; a great statue or picture grows under the power of the artist as a child in the mother's womb; and the very mind which directs the hands in formation is incapable of accounting to itself for the origin, the gradations, or the media of the process.

Poetry is the record of the best and happiest [144] moments of the happiest and best minds. We are aware of evanescent visitations of thought and feeling sometimes associated with place or person, sometimes regarding our own mind alone, and always arising unforeseen and departing unbidden, but elevating and delightful beyond all expression: so that even in the desire and the regret they leave, there cannot but be pleasure, participating as it does in the nature of its object. It is as it were the interpenetration of a diviner nature through our own; but its footsteps are like those of a wind over a sea, which the coming [145] calm erases, and whose traces remain only, as on the wrinkled sand which paves it. [146] These and corresponding conditions of being are

---

[143]

> . . . my Celestial Patroness, who deignes
> Her nightly visitation unimplor'd,
> And dictates to me slumbering, or inspires
> Easie my unpremeditated Verse.
> (*Paradise Lost*, IX, 21–24)

Cf. Shelley's reference to the "unpremediated art" of the skylark ("The a Skylark," 5).

[144] MSS A and D: happiest and best.

[145] 1840, Forman: morning.

[146] This language is reminiscent of Shelley's early "Hymn to Intellectual Beauty" (1816). Cf. also the "Essay on Christianity": "There

experienced principally by those of the most delicate sensibility and the most enlarged imagination; and the state of mind produced by them is at war with every base desire. The enthusiasm of virtue, love, patriotism, and friendship, is essentially linked with these emotions; and whilst they last, self appears as what it is, an atom to a Universe.[147] Poets are not only subject to these experiences as spirits of the most refined organisation, but they can colour all that they combine with the evanescent hues of this ethereal world; a word, or a trait in the representation of a scene or a passion, will touch the enchanted chord, and reanimate, in those who have ever experienced these emotions, the sleeping, the cold, the buried image of the past. Poetry thus makes immortal all that is best and most beautiful in the world; it arrests the vanishing apparitions which haunt the interlunations of life, and veiling them, or in language or in form, sends them forth among mankind, bearing sweet news of kindred joy to those with whom their sisters abide—abide, because there is no portal of expression from the caverns of the spirit which they inhabit into the universe of things. Poetry redeems from decay the visitations of the divinity in Man.

is a Power by which we are surrounded, like the atmosphere in which some motionless lyre is suspended, which visits with its breath our silent chords at will" (*Shelley's Prose*, p. 202). Shelley wrote Peacock that when he received "The Four Ages" he was reading Plato's *Ion.* Cf. his own translation: "For the authors of those great poems which we admire do not attain to excellence through the rules of any art, but they utter their beautiful melodies of verse in a state of inspiration, and, as it were, *posessed* by a spirit not their own" (533). A version of a latter section of this same passage appears in the manuscript of Shelley's draft of "A Defence of Poetry" (Koszul, pp. 121–122).

147 Cf. Milton in *The Reason of Church Government:* "These [poetic] abilities, wheresoever they be found, are the inspired gift of God, rarely bestowed, but yet to some (though most abuse) in every nation; and are of power, beside the office of a pulpit, to imbreed and cherish in a great people the seeds of virtue and public civility, to allay the perturbations of the mind, and set the affections in right tune" (Introduction to the Second Book). Shelley wrote to John and Maria Gisborne on July 7, 1820, asking that his own set of Milton's prose works be sent to him at Leghorn.

Poetry turns all things to loveliness; it exalts the beauty of that which is most beautiful, and it adds beauty to that which is most deformed; it marries exultation and horror, grief and pleasure, eternity and change; it subdues to union under its light yoke, all irreconcilable things. It transmutes all that it touches, and every form moving within the radiance of its presence is changed by wondrous sympathy to an incarnation of the spirit which it breathes; its secret alchemy turns to potable gold the poisonous waters which flow from death through life; it strips the veil of familiarity from the world, and lays bare the naked and sleeping beauty, which is the spirit of its forms.[148]

All things exist as they are perceived; at least in relation to the percipient.[149] "The mind is its own place, and of itself can make a Heaven of Hell, a Hell of Heaven." [150] But poetry defeats the curse which binds us to be subjected to the accident of surrounding impressions. And whether it spreads its own figured curtain, or withdraws life's dark veil from before the scene of things, it equally creates for us a being within our being. It makes us the inhabitants of a world to which the familiar world is a chaos. It reproduces the common Universe of which we are portions and percipients, and it purges from our inward sight the film of familiarity which obscures from us the wonder of our

[148] Coleridge said that in the *Lyrical Ballads* Wordsworth sought "to excite a feeling analogous to the supernatural, by awakening the mind's attention from the lethargy of custom, and directing it to the loveliness and the wonders of the world before us; an inexhaustible treasure, but for which, in consequence of the film of familiarity and selfish solicitude we have eyes, yet see not, ears that hear not, and hearts that neither feel nor understand" (*Biographia Literaria*, Chap. XIV). Cf. "The Witch of Atlas," stanza lxvi, and "Essay on Life": "The mist of familiarity obscures from us the wonder of our being" (*Shelley's Prose*, p. 172).

[149] Cf. "Essay on Life": "I confess that I am one of those who am unable to refuse my assent to the conclusions of those philosophers who assert that nothing exists but as it is perceived" (*Shelley's Prose*, p. 173). He believed, however, that the mind of the percipient made its own contribution: see "Mont Blanc," 4–6.

[150] *Paradise Lost*, I, 254–255.

being. It compels us to feel that which we perceive, and to imagine that which we know. It creates anew the universe, after it has been annihilated in our minds by the recurrence of impressions blunted by reiteration. It justifies that bold and true word of Tasso: *Non merita nome di creatore, se non Iddio ed il Poeta.*[151]

A poet, as he is the author to others of the highest wisdom, pleasure, virtue and glory, so he ought personally to be the happiest, the best, the wisest, and the most illustrious of men. As to his glory, let Time be challenged to declare whether the fame of any other institutor of human life be comparable to that of a poet. That he is the wisest, the happiest,[152] and the best, inasmuch as he is a poet, is equally incontrovertible: the greatest Poets have been men of the most spotless virtue, of the most consummate prudence, and, if we could look into the interior of their lives, the most fortunate of men: and the exceptions, as they regard those who possessed the imaginative[153] faculty in a high yet inferior degree, will be found on consideration to confirm[154] rather than destroy the rule. Let us for a moment stoop to the arbitration of popular breath, and usurping and uniting in our own persons the incompatible characters of accuser, witness, judge and executioner, let us without trial, testimony, or form, determine that[155] certain

151 "None deserves the name of creator except God and the Poet." Shelley quotes this saying in "Essay on Life," and slightly different versions of it in letters to Peacock (August 16, 1818) and Leigh Hunt (November 14–18, 1819). D. L. Clark points out that the quotation is not verbatim from Tasso but derives from his *Discorsi del Poema Eroico;* he suggests that Shelley took it from John C. Hobhouse's *Historical Illustrations of the Fourth Canto of Childe Harold* (1818), p. 26 (*Shelley's Prose*, p. 172n.).

152 Wordsworth and Coleridge would agree. Wordsworth called poets "the happiest of all men" (*Works*, p. 701) and Coleridge ascribes the loss of his poetic powers to his loss of "joy" ("Dejection: an Ode," stanza v).

153 MS D, 1840, 1845, Forman: poetic.

154 MS D, 1845: confine.

155 MS D, 1840, 1845, Forman: let us decide without trial, testimony, or form, that.

motives of those who are "there sitting where we dare not soar," [156] are reprehensible. Let us assume that Homer was a drunkard that Virgil was a flatterer, that Horace was a coward, that Tasso was a madman, that Lord Bacon was a peculator, that Raphael was a libertine, that Spenser was a poet laureate.[157] It is inconsistent with this division of our subject to cite living poets, but Posterity has done ample justice to the great names now referred to. Their errors have been weighed and found to have been dust in the balance; if their sins were as scarlet, they are now white as snow: [158] they have been washed in the blood of the mediator and the redeemer, Time. Observe in what a ludicrous chaos the imputations of real or fictitious crime have been confused in the contemporary calumnies against poetry and poets; consider how little is, as it appears—or appears, as it is; look to your own motives, and judge not, lest ye be judged.[159]

Poetry, as has been said, in this respect differs from logic, that it is not subject to the controul of the active powers of the mind, and that its birth and recurrence

[156] Cf. *Paradise Lost*, IV, 829. Shelley applies the idea to Keats in *Adonais*, xxxviii.

[157] The laureateship was not then in high repute, having been held from 1790 to 1813 by Henry James Pye and being currently in the possession of Robert Southey, whom the liberals considered a renegade. See Byron's *The Vision of Judgment*.

[158] MS D, 1840, 1845, Forman put the passage from "were" to "snow" in quotation marks, but it is only a paraphrase of Isaiah 1:18. The end of the paragraph is compounded of scriptural echoes: see also Daniel 5:27, Isaiah 40:15, Revelation 7:14, Hebrews 9:15 and 12:24, Colossians 4:5, and Matthew 7:1.

[159] Shelley was naturally sensitive about society's judgment of poets and played with this passage. His draft reads: "And in judging Poets, the interpreters & creators of all religion & philosophy, look into your own hearts, & examine if as ye are ignobler, so ye are better even than the conception which you can form of the defects of the great; & then if ye would be judged, judge" (Koszul, p. 114n.). His fair copy contains the canceled passage: "There is a certain plausibility in every erroneous opinion that has gained any degree of prevalence . . . notion of the immorality of poets" (*Julian*, VII, 357).

has no necessary connexion with consciousness or will.[160] It is presumptuous to determine that these are the necessary conditions of all mental causation, when mental effects are experienced insusceptible of being referred to them. The frequent recurrence of the poetical power, it is obvious to suppose, may produce in the mind an habit of order and harmony correlative with its own nature and with its effects upon other minds. But in the intervals of inspiration, and they may be frequent without being durable, a Poet becomes a man, and is abandoned to the sudden reflux of the influences under which others habitually live. But as he is more delicately organized than other men, and sensible to pain and pleasure, both his own and that of others, in a degree unknown to them, he will avoid the one and pursue the other with an ardour proportioned to this difference.[161] And he renders himself obnoxious to calumny, when he neglects to observe the circumstances under which these objects of universal pursuit and flight have disguised themselves in one another's garments.

But there is nothing necessarily evil in this error, and thus cruelty, envy, revenge, avarice, and the passions purely evil, have never formed any portion of the popular imputations on the lives of poets.

I have thought it most favourable to the cause of truth to set down these remarks according to the order in which they were suggested to my mind, by a consideration of the subject itself, instead of following that of the treatise that excited me to make them public.[162] Thus although devoid of

160 Coleridge held that the secondary imagination was "co-existing with the conscious will" (*Biographia Literaria*, Chap. XIII), but Wordsworth agrees, "Nor is it I who play the part./But a shy spirit in my heart,/That comes and goes" ("The Waggoner," 209–211).

161 Wordsworth also held that poets were "possessed of more than usual organic sensibility" ("Preface," *Works*, p. 735).

162 The references to "The Four Ages" are canceled in MS D, which then reads, as do 1840, 1845, Forman: instead of observing the formality of a polemical reply; but if the view which they contain be just, they will be found a refutation of the arguers against poetry, so far at least

the formality of a polemical reply; if the view they contain be just, they will be found to involve a refutation of the doctrines of the Four Ages of Poetry, so far at least as regards the first division of the subject. I can readily conjecture what should have moved the gall of the learned and intelligent author of that paper; I confess myself, like him, unwilling to be stunned by the Theseids of the hoarse Codri of the day. Bavius and Maevius undoubtedly are, as they ever were, insufferable persons.[163] But it belongs to a philosophical critic to distinguish rather than confound.

The first part of these remarks has related to Poetry in its elements and principles; and it has been shewn, as well as the narrow limits assigned them would permit, that what is called poetry, in a restricted sense, has a common source with all other forms of order and of beauty, according to which the materials of human life are susceptible of being arranged, and which is Poetry in an universal sense.

The second part will have for its object an application

---

as regards the first division of the subject. I can readily conjecture what should have moved the gall of some learned and intelligent writers who quarrel with certain versifiers; I confess myself, like them [1840, Forman: I, like them, confess].

[163] Cf. Shelley's comments in a letter to Peacock (March 21, 1821): "The Bavii & Maevii of the day are very fertile: & I wish those who honour me with boxes would read & inwardly digest your 'Four Ages of Poetry'; for I had much rather, for my private reading, receive political geological & moral treatises than this stuff in terza, ottava, & tremilesima rima, whose earthly baseness has attracted the lightning of your undiscriminating censure upon the temples of immortal song.—Proctor's verses enrage me far more than those of Codrus did Juvenal: & with better reason; Juvenal need not have been stunned unless he had liked it, but my boxes are packed with this trash to the exclusion of what I want to see." Codrus, Bavius, and Maevius are bywords for feeble poetasters who owe their immortality to having infuriated their betters. Juvenal is aroused to retaliation against the "Theseid of Cordus hoarse from reciting" (Satire I. 1–2) and Virgil and Horace both ridiculed Bavius and Maevius (Eclogue III. 90; Epode X. 1–2). William Gifford, editor of the Quarterly Review from 1809 to 1824, applied the terms to contemporary writers in his The Baviad (1794) and The Maeviad (1795), in which he attacked the Della Cruscans and the current dramatists.

of these principles to the present state of the cultivation of Poetry, and a defence of the attempt to idealize the modern forms of manners and opinions, and compel them into a subordination to the imaginative and creative faculty.[164] For the literature of England,[165] an energetic development of which has ever preceded or accompanied a great and free development of the national will, has arisen as it were from a new birth. In spite of the low-thoughted envy which would undervalue contemporary merit, our own will be a memorable age in intellectual achievements, and we live among such philosophers and poets as surpass beyond comparison any who have appeared since the last national struggle for civil and religious liberty. The most unfailing herald, companion, and follower of the awakening of a great people to work a beneficial change in opinion or institution, is Poetry. At such periods there is an accumulation of the power of communicating and receiving intense and impassioned conceptions respecting man and nature. The persons in whom this power resides, may often as far as regards many portions of their nature, have little apparent correspondence with that spirit of good of which they are the ministers.[166] But even whilst they deny and abjure, they are yet compelled to serve, the Power which is seated upon the throne of their own soul. It is impossible to read the compositions of the most celebrated writers of

[164] Shelley never wrote the projected second part.

[165] From "For the literature of England" to the end of the essay is adapted from Shelley's *A Philosophical View of Reform*, probably written 1819–1820 (*Shelley's Prose*, pp. 239–240).

[166] Shelley is probably thinking of Robert Southey and William Wordsworth, whom he found guilty of playing the renegade from their youthful radical positions and becoming administrative toadies. In 1819 he made fun of Wordsworth in *Peter Bell the Third*, although Mary Shelley declared in a note to that poem: "No man ever admired Wordsworth's poetry more;—he read it perpetually, and taught others to appreciate its beauties." Shelley's "I thought of thee, fair Celandine" compares the withered flower to Wordsworth: "Fallen on a cold and evil time;/His heart is gone" (30–31) (W. E. Peck, *Shelley, His Life and Work* [Boston, 1927], I, 478).

the present day without being startled with the electric
life which burns within their words. They measure the
circumference and sound the depths of human nature with
a comprehensive and all-penetrating spirit, and they are
themselves perhaps the most sincerely astonished at its
manifestations; for it is less their spirit than the spirit of the
age.[167] Poets are the hierophants of an unapprehended in-
spiration; the mirrors of the gigantic shadows which futurity
casts upon the present; the words which express what they
understand not; the trumpets which sing to battle, and
feel not what they inspire; the influence which is moved
not, but moves. Poets are the unacknowledged legislators
of the world.

[167] William Hazlitt called his collection of critical essays on his con-
temporaries *The Spirit of the Age* (1825).

The Library of Liberal Arts

Below is a representative selection from The Library of Liberal Arts. This partial listing—taken from the more than 200 scholarly editions of the world's finest literature and philosophy—indicates the scope, nature, and concept of this distinguished series.